JOY
24 x 7

$$\frac{JOY}{24 \times 7}$$

JOY
24 x 7

Jeetendra Jain
explores Joy with

SADHGURU

www.joy24x7.com

JAICO PUBLISHING HOUSE

Ahmedabad Bangalore Bhopal Chennai
Delhi Hyderabad Kolkata Mumbai

Published by Jaico Publishing House
A-2, Jash Chambers, Sir Phirozshah Mehta Road
Fort, Mumbai - 400 001
jaicopub@jaicobooks.com
www.jaicobooks.com

JOY 24 X 7
ISBN 978-81-7992-914-8

First Jaico Impression: 2008
Second Jaico Impression: 2008

Printed by
Rashmi Graphics
#3, Amrutwel CHS Ltd., C.S. #50/74
Ganesh Galli, Lalbaug, Mumbai-400 012
E-mail: tiwarijp@vsnl.net

Contents

Why no Joy?

Joy is here!

A Note On The Book

"If you just understand the fact that you're either joyful or miserable only by choice, the question is only whether you make your choices consciously or unconsciously. If you're aware of this, yes, any moment when you understand it is you who is creating misery and not somebody else, you would definitively stop it."

These words from Sadhguru Jaggi Vasudev have changed my complete perception of Joy. Till then, I had all kinds of hallucinatory ideas about Joy (and still do) but the 2 days that I spent with him, seeking his thoughts on Joy showed me a whole new world.

While I would like to talk about Sadhguru, the "Guru" and the dispeller of darkness, whose power helped me realize a new dimension of Joy which I had not experienced until now, the dimension which is so much beyond... I would love to talk about Sadhguru the man.

As a man he is the most Joyful. He is so much 100% in the moment in whatever he does — intense and involved. A fascinating story-teller, he has the most incredible sense of humour and presents the deepest concepts most lucidly through his by now famous anecdotes. He is an amazing person to have a discussion with on any topic ranging from frisbees to books to BMW bikes to politics. He is quite incisive and has great clarity about anything he speaks. He can make anything sound simple. His precision with words and the ability to put across the most profound thought in a way that "you" will understand is most precious for the listener.

Sadhguru, the man, is most playful. Watch him when he makes twenty people chase the Frisbee that he has flung with his intensity. He is humility personified and you can feel it when he serves you food with his own hands. When he is talking you, he is talking only to you. He talks about his most incredible achievements with so much simplicity as though he were talking about his morning walk.

These aspects of Sadhguru as the human being are a source of inspiration for me and a source of Joy. Sadhguru, that dimension beyond the human being I see, is Joy itself.

This book is a journey about Joy.

It is not a guidebook. It is not a "how to" book. It is not going to give you "an instant formula for Joy". On the contrary it is going to make you restless to seek Joy, as it has done for me. It will change the context of your life.

I have not written this book. I am only a fortunate medium for what Sadhguru has to say since I wanted to share this Joy with so many people around the world like you. The parts in the book which are about the characters Dev, Lila and Arya have been written by me. Sadhguru's words on Joy begin with a marking of his name in each chapter.

No matter what your circumstances are, I wish you boundless Joy that this creation has to offer. It is your birthright and all you need is openness to seek it!

Actually you have no option but to seek Joy, no option but to choose Joy.

May Joy be with you, always!

—Jeetendra Jain
August 20, 2008

Special mentions of some Joyful people

There are several people whose names have to be mentioned and these individuals thanked simply because they have helped make this book happen.

Swami Nisarga has been handholding this book through so many roles – as a motivator, as an editor, as a critic and as a co-ordinator for this project at the Ashram. Shobha Kadur quietly edited this book many times over and with much Joy and patience. Hoda Durham helped nail the process to the elusive last chapter. Swami Devasatwa for his patience while helping design the book. Maa Gambhiri for helping co-ordinate and linking up with the publishers.

Mr. Ashwin Shah, Akash Shah and Mr. R.H. Sharma of Jaico publishers need to be thanked for their whole-hearted involvement in the vision for this book and for bringing the book out in an incredibly short time.

Vivek of Vivek Sahni Design, New Delhi and their team for magical cover design of the book and the inside pages.

Preeti Vyas and her young dynamic team at Depot (Big Bazaar) for encouraging this effort so well without knowing much about us.

For Kumar at the Ashram for his tremendous efforts in the launch of the book. Swami Udhava for his dogged efforts in the last stages before the book publishing.

For many Isha Yoga meditators, who joyfully became a part of this process of developing ideas for the book including sessions with Sadhguru : Kavita Pasricha, Revathi Shivkumar, Tina, Natalie, Angela, Maa Kashyapi, Swami Ullasa. My friends Gangadharan Menon, Sabina Verma and scores of other well wishers who motivated me and helped the efforts on this book.

For Ashok Jain and several employees at Oxygen Communications in Mumbai for helping on the book designs, initial conceptualisation, etc.

For my wife and Isha meditator, Shilpa and my daughter Isha for their joyful and constant support for this book and in this journey.

Their small and large inputs have made the journey of putting this book together a very joyful one.

What is Joy?

What is the way out?

"What is Joy, Dad? Are all of us joyful?" asked Arya, the 6-year old son of Dev & Lila with a very innocent look in his eyes. His parents were stumped with this question and could only exchange a bewildered look.

Arya was a fun loving, mischievous and playful child who often had a bagful of wonderful and innocent questions for his parents which occasionally brought a smile to their otherwise burdened life of ambitions and responsibility.

This time, Arya immediately knew that his parents could not really answer the question. So, he went on happily to his room to play with his new whirring top even as Dev and Lila stared blankly at the poster displayed in Arya's room which said, "THE WAY OUT IS THROUGH THE IN DOOR!". Neither Dev nor Arya liked this poster nor knew what it meant. A friend at Isha Yoga had got them this poster and Arya liked it very much for some unknown reason.

The question that Arya had asked his father and mother seemed to play on their minds for several months.

You are a Joy industry

Dev and Lila were smiling at the little toy that Arya was playing with which was a mechanically wound toy shaped like a monkey that would clap and smile.

"No matter which direction you set this toy and let it go it seems to smile and clap. Dad" said a beaming Arya.

"Surely son" said Lila " and the day it stops doing this, you will not play with the toy anymore. Isn't that true?"

Arya laughed.

Sadhguru: Let us pose a question – In the last 24 hours, how many moments of Joy have you known? Every person should constantly look at it, at the end of the day. Every night before going to bed, spend just 5-10 minutes checking your accounts – how many moments of Joy have I known today? From yesterday to today has it improved or has it fallen? Are my Joys in profit or loss? Do this like a checkout everyday.

Right now if you look at your life, everything that you are doing is in pursuit of Joy, so you are a Joy industry. If you are a Joy industry you need to check if from the age of 5 your production has been improving or depleting.

When you were a child, other people considered you a child but actually you were a slave because you just obeyed commands. If somebody said 'stand up', you stood up. If somebody said 'sleep', you slept and if somebody said 'go to school', you went to school.

They thought you were a child but in your experience, you were a slave who was so terribly eager to grow up soon. Now that you have grown up, have got your own life, your own bank account, your own stuff going and everything of your own, has your Joy multiplied? It has got subtracted or divided, isn't it?

Please see, everything that you did is in pursuit of Joy. Whether you went for a job, sought a career, built businesses, made money or built families, everything has been in pursuit of your Joy. So when the basic thing doesn't happen, you are badly caught up in the process. It is like the example of running a power loom. When we want to manufacture cloth we work round the clock and put in a lot of raw material, but when we don't find any end product generated, what do we do with the unit?

We shut it down or overhaul it – that's all the choice that you have. Either the loom needs to be shut down, or it needs to be overhauled, that's all.

Right now, if you look at your life, everything that you are doing is in pursuit of Joy. In other words, you are a Joy industry!

Square one of your life

"Such a wonderful tree, Mom!" shouted Arya when he looked up at the huge banyan tree in the garden.

"Yes such huge branches and such beautiful leaves," added Lila.

"And such a huge trunk mom, it's so wonderful!" Arya said while hugging the tree trunk fondly.

"But my son, do you see what supports all this?" Lila asked Arya and then pointed to some of the roots of the tree that had sprung above the ground

Arya looked at them curiously.

Sadhguru: Joy is not the end of the world. I am talking about Joy as the square one of your life, as a solid foundation for your life to flower upon.

I am not talking about Joy as the ultimate possibility in your life; I am talking about Joy as the 'A' of your life, not the 'Z' of your life. When the 'A' has not happened, what else are you talking about? You are trying to build a house without laying the foundations. Do you know what a feat it will be to hold up a house that doesn't have foundations? If you let it go for one moment, it will fall on your head. That's how your life is, isn't it? If you are off guard for one moment, everything will crash upon your head.

But if you have a solid foundation of Joy, you can do whatever you want to do on that. You can even build a huge mansion and it is fine because it has got good foundations. Now you have no foundations or you have shaky foundations and you are trying to hold the building up. What a torture every little activity of life must be!

I am not talking about Joy as the ultimate possibility in your life; I am talking about Joy as the 'A' of your life, not the 'Z' of your life.

Phantom strikes again!

Lila was very annoyed with Arya and did not know what to do with the cookies that she had bought at the supermarket.

Each time she bought cookies and hid them, Arya would sniff them out. Even if she lied that she had not bought any cookies, Arya would quickly find them and would consume a good half of them before she found out.

Lila felt that her delight of buying cookies would never last.

Sadhguru: The whole science and wisdom of what we refer to as inner nature or inner engineering or inner sciences, means, not seeing Joy as something that we could achieve in our life but seeing Joy as the very basis of our lives.

Is this the only goal of our life? Joy is not the goal; it is the square one of your life. Other things can happen, only if this one thing happens. Otherwise, you'll live constantly with the fear of misery striking at you. Anything can happen to you at any moment, that's the way of life.

Externally, physically just about anything can happen. Right now you're in existence but the next moment you may evaporate. It is a possibility. We're not wishing it, but it is a possibility (Laughs). But more than what can happen externally, your fear and your concern about what can happen within you is your experience of you becoming miserable, anxious, or stressed. These are your concerns, and no matter how you try to handle it, misery keeps striking back again and again.

Once a kindergarten teacher walked into the classroom and found a muddy puddle, right in the middle of the classroom, intentionally made by somebody. She looked at it and asked 'Who made this mess in the class?' None of the tiny tots opened their mouths because they had a certain camaraderie about not squealing.

The teacher asked again, but nobody answered. The teacher then thought there is no point pushing it, so she said, "Now boys and girls, we will all close our eyes and give whoever made this mess five minutes, to just clean it up, go back and sit. Nobody needs to know who did it, but this mess must be cleaned up".

Everybody closed their eyes and suddenly the teacher heard a patter of feet, the bucket and some other noises. She gave this enough time. After some time they again heard the patter of feet running back and sitting down. Everything was quiet and that meant the job was done. When everybody opened their eyes, they found one more muddy pool, and alongside it was written 'Phantom strikes again!'.

So, every time in your life, at every stage in your life, you think 'Oh if I just get this job, this is it, my life is made' but a little while later, it strikes back. You thought 'If I get married to this particular person, that's it, my life is made', and it strikes back like hell! (Laughs).

At every stage you think 'this is it', but life always strikes back again and again, isn't it? Life strikes back not because there is something wrong with creation, but because you're not in tune with your own basic existence, because you have got identified with petty things that you gathered. You have become an accumulation, you have no existence of your own.

At every stage, you think 'this is it', but life strikes back again and again because you are not in tune with your own basic existence.

The fruit of action

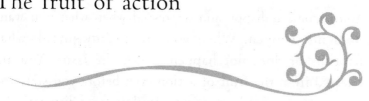

Dev would never find Lila free for a chat. Her mornings were busy with preparing breakfast and other household chores while late evenings were spent in winding up for the day. Even her weekends were busy with shopping or helping Arya with his school assignments.

"You are never free Lila ...to talk to me," grumbled Dev.

"Oh come on Dev" smiled Lila "you can never see me free even if I am, because you are always grumbling!"

Sadhguru: Right now, you are living on the surface, so every contradiction that happens around you, upsets your inner experience.

Life is nurturing you with such a deep sense of Joy that if you were rooted into the core of life, then outside situations would have no impact on you.

You can handle the outside situations only to the best of your capability. Some things happen the way you want them, some things don't happen the way you want them. What about it? That's how life is, and you have no issue with it. Some things work for you, some things don't work for you. Even if it doesn't work for you, obviously it is working for somebody else. Isn't it? What's the hassle?

You become unhappy and depressed when what you want does not happen. When you are already joyful, what happens or does not happen is not the issue. You are released from the fruit of action even before you start the action. This is not because you develop some dispassion or renunciation about it but simply because you are so joyful. If you do not know Joy within yourself as a way of being, you cannot be free from the fruit of action because the fruit of action is the source of your Joy. How can you be free from it? You cannot be free from it.

If you do not know Joy within yourself as a way of being, you cannot be free from the fruit of action because the fruit of action is the source of your Joy.

The collector's item

"Why do you collect these stupid marbles Arya" Dev asked his son who had a box full of assorted marbles.

Arya thought for a moment and then retorted "But Dad these are better than those funny pictures of football and cricket players that you collect...and you were very angry when I once sat on your collection book!"

Lila who had just stepped into the room laughed and Arya immediately admonished her too saying, "...and Mom don't you laugh! You collect all those old recipes for your kitchen too and you were so upset when I dropped ketchup on them...!"

Sadhguru: The problem is that you get identified with the accumulations. Accumulation can enrich your life: in any sphere of life, who is the rich man? The one who has accumulated plenty, isn't it? So accumulation is not the problem, it enriches your life. But, you're identified with your accumulations and since you can only accumulate things, you have reduced yourself into a thing.

I know you accumulate people, but they are also things in your experience, because they're your property isn't it?

People are your property. Your husband or your wife, your children, they are your property. Somehow, because accumulating inanimate things is not sufficient for your ego, you accumulate animate things; otherwise you don't feel good. They may be living beings, but in your experience, they're just things that you possess.

So accumulation by itself is not the problem, your getting identified with it and your reducing yourself into a thing, is the problem. It is in this identification and reducing yourself into a thing that you have lost the experience of this being. You live as if this being doesn't exist, only accumulation exists, because you get identified with it.

If you do not identify yourself with any aspect of your accumulation, you still have an existence, a very large sense of existence, a very powerful sense of existence without any accumulation. But you chose to identify yourself because you never allowed yourself to taste the vastness of your existence for a moment.

You identified with one thing, and you became that and it felt insufficient after some time. So you accumulated one more thing. That too felt good only for some time and then it felt insufficient. So you accumulate one more thing, one more thing, and one more thing.

If you gather all the galaxies into your accumulation, you will still feel insufficient because there is something within you, which will not settle for any little thing, because its nature is that of the creator himself. That which is within you, which is the basis of creation cannot be limited to any particular identification.

The moment you tie it down with an identity, it struggles. This struggle is what you're experiencing as lack of Joy or misery. If you untie it from all identities, joyfulness is not something that you run after. Joyfulness is an attainment that you're looking up to. It is not a fruit hanging from the sky that you reach out for, it is something that will naturally play at your feet.

> *If you gather all the galaxies into your accumulation, you will still feel insufficient because there is something within you, which will not settle for any little thing, because its nature is that of the creator himself.*

An outside chance

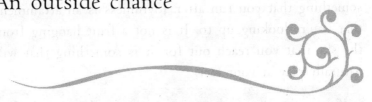

Lila's mood changed. She suddenly looked delighted after being so dull the whole day.

When Dev asked her why she suddenly felt good, Lila pointed out at the rain and said "Rains always cheer me up".

"So we will get you under the water spray the next time you are in a foul mood" said a visibly upset Dev. "And if that is not the real thing then Arya and I will go up to the roof and sprinkle water with our lawn sprayer" he added with an impish smile. Arya was laughing and he ran out to play in the rain.

Arya then opened an umbrella and held it over Lila's head and this made her smile. She realized it had been so stupid of her to wait for the rain so that she could smile.

Sadhguru: If there is no foundation of Joy, I cannot do what I intend to do with people. So irrespective of who you are, where you are or what you are, I'm constantly laying the foundation which you're always trying to uproot! (Laughs). Laying up the foundation is not in terms of teaching, not in terms of understanding.

Joy is not because you know something, Joy is not because you understand something, Joy is because the deepest core of you functions, finds expression. When you sit with me, my energies are such, your physical body, mind and your emotions get naturally aligned in a certain way, so you feel joyful.

But, you need to understand this, even though the induction is from outside, the actual Joy is always from within. In poetry we would say 'I will shower Joy upon you'. But, no, we cannot shower Joy upon you. We can create a situation where you cannot help being aligned in a certain way whereby, you naturally feel joyful. Joy is always an inner experience, if it was showered upon you, your skin should feel it first, but that's not how it happens. It is a certain alignment within you, which naturally allows the innermost core to find expression and Joy happens.

There's nothing else wrong with people except that they're miserable, isn't it? (Laughs) They are miserable in whatever they do and they don't do. If they get to do something they make themselves miserable, if they don't, they become miserable. They just need an excuse.

But you will see if you're in a certain level of alignment on a particular day, suddenly you will find all you need is an excuse to burst into laughter. But if you're in a certain level of misalignment, all you need is an excuse to burst into tears and depression. So you need to understand, whatever you are thinking right now as the source of your Joy is just an excuse.

> *There's nothing else wrong with people except that they're miserable, if they get to do something they make themselves miserable, if they don't, they become miserable. They just need an excuse!*

Somehow, sometime

Dev had a colleague who was having a tough time with his boss.

Each time his boss hollered and asked him for an update on a project, the colleague would run around the department looking for information and come back with some sketchy details. Even though the work was going on at the required pace, his boss was seldom happy with the status of the project.

Every time the boss heard from his colleague "Somehow we will do it sir!" the boss's face would turn red with anger. He did not like the term "somehow".

"Somehow you may have to find another job!" he would retort when he heard this rather naïve reassurance that his junior gave. Dev found this very amusing after a while and he smiled at this routine.

Sadhguru: Generally people look at their Joy emotionally. I want you to look at this technically because emotions are fine and juicy but you can't recreate them. If you try to recreate them, they will become pretentious and painful. If you look at it technically, if you understand the mechanics of Joy, then you can create it all the time. So right now, in so many ways you're trying to bullshit yourself into Joy, but it is not working.

Can I tell you a joke? Are you okay? You are so serious, I'm afraid to even tell you a joke. On a certain day, a bull and a pheasant who were partners were grazing on a field. The bull was grazing while the pheasant was picking ticks off the bull. The pheasant looked up at a huge tree on the edge of the field and very nostalgically said, "Alas! There was a time when I could fly to the topmost branch of the tree. Now I don't have strength in my wings to even fly to the lowest branch of the tree."

The bull very nonchalantly said, "That's no problem. Just eat a little bit of my dung and within a fortnight you will reach the topmost branch of the tree." The pheasant said, "Come on! What kind of nonsense is that?" The bull replied, "Really! Try and see! The whole humanity is on it." The pheasant very hesitantly pecked at the dung and lo! On the very first day it reached the lowest branch of the tree.

In a fortnight's time it did reach the topmost branch of the tree. It went and sat on the topmost branch of the tree and trilled and looked around, enjoying the scenery. An old farmer, who saw the fat old pheasant on the topmost branch of the tree pulled out his shotgun and shot the bird down.

So the moral of the story is: many times, even bullshit can get you to the top, but it never lets you stay there. It never lets you stay there isn't it? That's what you're trying to do with your happiness, to be happy somehow. One moment up there, one moment there, down. You cannot get there like that.

So, your Joy keeps crashing down repeatedly. It doesn't matter how many times you think 'This is it', it keeps falling down simply because you don't understand the mechanics of it. You're just trying to get there somehow but you can't get there somehow. If you want to get there, if you want to do something, if you want to create a certain result either externally or internally, you must be able to do the right thing.

If you do not do the right thing, then it doesn't happen. The problem with people is that they think that they can do it somehow, both with the external and the internal. It doesn't work like that.

> *Your Joy keeps crashing down repeatedly. It doesn't matter how many times you think 'This is it', it keeps falling down simply because you don't understand the mechanics of it.*

A shorcut to Joy

Dev would always drive to the supermarket with Lila by a different route each time and Lila found this odd.

"Why don't you just take the main road to the supermarket Dev?" enquired a puzzled Lila.

"I. ...Well enjoy these different routes Lila," said a hesitant Dev.

"Well you seem to be mostly troubled when you take these routes trying to avoid the pedestrians, bicycle riders and the little children.... Why can't you take a simple straight route and smile?" Lila asked a calm Dev.

Sadhguru: Why are you seeking Joy? Hmm, I don't know why you are seeking Joy. Neither I nor anybody else asked you to seek Joy. It is not because of me or someone else that you're seeking Joy, the life within you is constantly seeking Joy, and it is not an idea or a philosophy.

This is the basic expression of existence. The mango tree is constantly longing to produce sweetness, nobody taught it to, that's how its nature is. So that's how all human nature is, seeking Joy.

It doesn't matter in how many ways you mess your mind; you're still pursuing Joy, isn't it? Whether you make it happen or not is questionable, but your pursuit is not questionable. Every human being is pursuing Joy. It doesn't matter how, whether you're seeking money, power, pleasure, alcohol, God or heaven, you're still in pursuit of Joy.

So, if you're doing everything in pursuit of Joy, all I'm asking is, instead of rooting it through so many things, why don't you address it directly? Is it not time that you address it directly? Instead of trying to go around the world and come back here?

A tourist came here and asked the local village boy how far Isha Yoga Center was. The boy replied 'It is twenty four thousand nine hundred and ninety six miles, if you go the way you're going right now, but if you turn around it is just four miles'. If you just turn around there are only four layers of the body to penetrate. If you go this way, it is twenty four thousand nine hundred and ninety six miles, the choice is yours.

Nothing wrong with this, just stupid and being stupid is not a crime.

If you're doing everything that you're doing in pursuit of Joy, all I'm asking is instead of rooting it through so many things, why don't you address it directly?

Just plain, dumb, stupid

Everything seemed to be going wrong for Dev that Monday. He just could not understand why everything was going wrong.... at work, on the road, with his colleagues.... it just seemed to be a very bad day.

That evening, he reached home exhausted, rang the doorbell and waited for Lila to open the door.

"What is the bad news Lila?" he asked her with a rather strange face and in frightful anticipation, even as she opened the door.

Lila was puzzled. She looked at him, estimated his problem and said "The bad news is about 5' 10" and is standing at the door right now!"

Sadhguru: If you made your life energies inert, that would be a good service to the world because you would be dead, but you have made your life energies a vigorously negative function, going in the wrong direction, taking on a wrong form; maybe wrong is not the word, an unpleasant form. Unhappiness means unpleasantness, isn't it?

So instead of keeping the physical body, mind and energy

pleasant, you have chosen to keep it unpleasant. If I ask you why, you will blame your mother-in-law, boss, wife, husband, child, bank balance or the hole in your pocket. However, none of these are the reasons, it is just that you're plain stupid. There is no other reason.

Especially if your mother-in-law is mean, and your boss is a tyrant and your wife is a bitch and your bank balance is empty, it is all the more important that you must keep pleasant the one thing that you have in your hands, isn't it? But everybody and everything has turned unpleasant.

All the time you blame other people. If people and situations around us are unpleasant, that's bad enough. You don't have to turn yourself, your own body, mind, and energies into unpleasantness. There is absolutely no intelligence in this. So one must know the one and only reason why one knows misery is because one is stupid. Just plain dumb, stupid; that's all. There is no other reason.

When people complain about their unhappiness they say – and this may sound arrogant, 'Oh! Do you know what's happening in my life? Yesterday I lost my this thing, tomorrow I'm going to lose something else.' I know all those things, everything that people can lose and gain; I have lost and gained in my life too.

Joyfulness doesn't happen because everything is perfect but joyfulness happens because you are unwilling to subjugate your intelligence to what is happening around you. Once your intelligence is entangled with the situations around you, once your intelligence is entangled because of the identities that you take on, then, it doesn't function any more. Misery is the only way then.

If you happen to be joyful, it is in spite of you; maybe it is some old food that you ate somewhere else. Past actions may still be working, old momentum still working somewhere. Something sensible that you did somewhere must be still working, but that won't last forever. The old food will rot after sometime. You have to make fresh food everyday if you want to have it all the time. You must learn to cook fresh food everyday.

If you manage to cook on one day and expect to eat the same food for the rest of your life, you will be eating manure after sometime, not food. That will invariably happen.

Joyfulness doesn't happen because everything is perfect but joyfulness happens because you are unwilling to subjugate your intelligence to what is happening around you.

Action replay

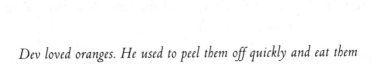

Dev loved oranges. He used to peel them off quickly and eat them and thoroughly enjoy the fruit.

On a certain day one of the oranges he ate was so unbearably sour he just could not eat it. "What a terrible orange Lila! How can an orange be so awful?" he cried.

"O come on Dev!" laughed Lila "how can an orange be good every time? Why don't you enjoy this bad orange too?" Dev was puzzled.

He picked one more orange from the basket, hoping this would be a good one. He wondered if it was about the orange or about him....

Sadhguru: Joyfulness is not an emotion, joyfulness is a certain way, a certain pleasantness that creeps into every aspect of your life, and that's why you're joyful. It is not that somebody told you a joke and you laughed. That is okay, a momentary Joy but it cannot last. You cannot be laughing at jokes all the time.

If at every moment of your life, somebody tells you a joke,

jokes will become absolutely sick, you know? It is like this with everything. Whether it is music, dance, love or relationships, they can become sick if you try to overdo any of those things. But, your being is never going to be sick, because that's the basis of your existence.

So if you bring this pleasantness into your being, joyfulness is the way you are. When you are like this, if you seek a relationship, you obviously want to share your Joy not to squeeze Joy out of somebody. Once you go out in the world, whether you work or you relate to somebody or whatever you do, the quality of your life is just very different when you share your Joy. You are no more in pursuit of Joy. There is a significant shift from pursuing Joy, to wanting to share Joy with people whose very basis of life it is. Once you are like this, you are no more a vested interest, you are not in compulsive action anymore; you will do what's needed.

Joyfulness is not an emotion, joyfulness is a certain way, a certain pleasantness that creeps into every aspect of your life, and that's why you're joyful.

First person Joy

After trying hard to paint a special Japanese flower for a couple of hours, Lila called Dev and Arya to comment on her flower painting.

"What exactly is this Lila?" Dev asked her trying to be polite while Arya screamed "Where is the flower mom?"

Lila was stunned by their response. She had no courage to tell them that she was trying to paint a Japanese flower she had never seen...

Sadhguru: How do you know what to create if you don't know what it is? In your experience, if there is no Joy, how will you create Joy for everybody else?

Now, let's say I make myself utterly miserable, crying my heart out but willing to work for all of you, to make you happy. In three days time, you will see that the ashram will be like a mourning place. Even now, maybe I am killing myself with my work but I am doing it joyfully, not as a service to anybody. I see that something needs to be done and I'm doing it, that's all. So it is not a burden on anybody.

If I cry everyday and make myself really miserable and continue to do so till I die, do you know what misery it will cause to everyone else? If I don't do anything they'll be fine according to their own nonsense. In the same way, if you do this kind of work without being joyful yourself, it'll cause more misery to everybody.

In a lot of families, a lot of so-called parents are doing this. They say, 'It doesn't matter how much we suffer, we want our children to be happy.' How are their children going to be happy when they set an example of suffering everyday? What you do at 30, your child will do at 20, you better know it. If these people became long-faced at the age of 30, the children become long-faced at the age of 20.

Whatever it may be, if you started smoking at 18, your son will smoke at 8. Suppose your father did not smoke, but in spite of that, you started smoking at 18 and your son watched you smoke; most probably by the time he is 8 or 10 years old, he will start smoking because he is always one step ahead. Almost everything that a child learns is by example.

If you do not set an example of Joy, and you only talk about Joy, it doesn't mean anything. It just doesn't mean anything. It is like a blind man talking about light. Ask the blind man to switch the light on. Now if you show him the switch he may press it, that's not the point, but if you ask him to create light, what kind of light will he create?

If he has never seen light and has no concept of light, he will believe you if you made a sound and told him it is light. That's what people are doing about Joy; they don't know what Joy is. They have been told that marriage is Joy. Marital bliss, OK? Although they have never known the bliss in their life, see how desperately they try to get their children married.

They themselves don't know why they're trying to get their children married, but they have to get them married because they believe that marriage is Joy. It is just like that light for the blind man isn't it? For a joyless man, what is Joy?

In your experience, if there is no Joy, how will you create Joy for everybody?

Visitation from Joy

Whenever Lila got a call from one of her friends in the evening, she was very delighted as it gave her a chance to gossip with them for long and then feel very good. Dev almost felt that she would wait eagerly for a call every evening and that she would feel fresh and energized after that.

One day she waited rather long and there was no phone call. Just then the doorbell rang and she was so delighted as it sounded like a phone call to her. This happened very often and then she realized that it was Dev who was playing this prank with Arya — who would ring the doorbell and vanish — just to replace her fascination for the telephone call....

Sadhguru: There are many people who feel joyful by drinking alcohol. It is true, that's why so many people drink. You better acknowledge that. Lots of people know a little Joy only on the weekend when they drink; otherwise the whole week is just a burden. Or when they drink every evening: the whole day is a burden and when they sip their drink in the evening they feel good. It is a reality for people. You cannot deny it, isn't it so?

Right now, we are talking about shifting our lives from having a visitation from Joy to being the very source of Joy. That's the thing we are talking about, because nobody can be drinking, painting, dancing or singing 24 hours. No particular action is possible for 24 hours. Joy is an inner situation. If you use any external activity to create an inner situation, you naturally get enslaved to that external activity, and that becomes the condition for your Joy.

If you are a painter and tomorrow your paint and brush are taken away, you cannot paint anymore. If life situations do it to you, then you will be extremely miserable and your whole reason will be 'I can't paint, that's why I'm miserable.'

Every day nature paints different colours, where is the need for you to add any paint to it? If you like to do it, it is ok you do it, but there is enough painting going on everyday, it is just that you have no eyes to see, isn't it? From morning to evening, do you see just how much painting is going on? Day and night somebody is constantly painting. You just have to look at it and enjoy it. If you stand there, it will paint you also, every which way you want.

So if you use any particular activity to create an inner situation in you, you will get enslaved with that particular activity deeply. That's the basis of your slavery and bondage; and unless you change that you will never know Joy as a way of being. You will have Joy only as a visitor in your life. That much is happening to everybody I hope.

Right now, we are talking about shifting our lives from having a visitation from Joy to being the very source of Joy.

If you use any external activity to create an inner situation, you naturally get enslaved to that external activity, and that becomes the condition for your Joy.

ᴋ of Joy

Dev and Arya loved watching spooky ghost movies on television at night because they wanted some deeper experience. One night they started seeing the movie with all lights turned off in the house. It was quite eerie. Yet another night, they shut all lights and also pulled down the curtains — it was an even deeper experience.

But the next time they found their experience had gone much deeper when they found the carpet beneath their feet moving slowly as they watched a spooky film on television. They froze in their seats on the sofa before they realized that it was Lila who was pulling the carpet with a long rope tied to one end of the carpet!

Sadhguru: Why do people consume alcohol? Why are people mad about sex? Why are people going for drugs? Why do people want to jump off mountains? Why do people want to do absolutely risky things in their lives? Sticking their necks out every day just to experience a little butterfly in their stomach, isn't it?

Somewhere every human being wants to know life in a deeper way than he knows it right now. Unfortunately, for most people pain is the deepest experience that they have known. Unpleasantness is the deepest experience in their life; they have never known true pleasantness within themselves. Pleasantness has just been on the surface while unpleasantness has been so deep rooted.

It is because of this, that people with some intensity like artists, musicians, painters and dancers have always sought pain as an expression because it gives depth to their work. Joy does not give depth to their work because they don't know how to depict Joy in its highest form, in its deepest possibility, because they have never known it. They have known pain, so they deepen their pain and try to depict that pain in work because at least there is depth to it. It is unpleasant, but there is depth to it.

And this depth, this trying to get a deep attraction into life is something that every human being is constantly trying to achieve. All the time people seek experiences deeper than what it presently is, isn't it?

Whether they come to the ashram or go to the bar, or to the cathouse or wherever they go, they seek a deeper experience somehow. Isn't it? Putting many aspects of their life to risk. If you go to the bar you are risking something, if you come to the ashram you are risking something, if you go to the cathouse you are risking something. Wherever you go, you seek a deeper experience of life. Somehow in the process you are putting your life to risk in so many ways, isn't it?

Whether people come to the ashram or go to the bar, or to the cathouse or wherever they go, they seek a deeper experience somehow. Isn't it?

Joyful fool

Dev had a friend at work who was a very simple man. One day Dev went up to him and asked him "How come you seem so simple and uncomplicated unlike most people around here? How do you manage to do this?"

His friend smiled at the compliment and said "I don't trouble my brains very often" he said, "and I just look at things the way they are."

Dev was more troubled now "How? Will you not lose your intelligence if you don't use it?"

His friend now said rather simply "Depends on what you don't want to lose"

Sadhguru: What's the connection between intelligence and Joy?

If you have made yourself truly joyful, you must be an intelligent person because that means you've fulfilled the fundamental purpose of your life. Maybe not the ultimate purpose, but at least you have fulfilled the fundamental purpose of your life.

In this world, whom do you call intelligent? Somebody who gets to fulfill what he wants to do; somebody who gets to win the game he wants to play; somebody who takes a particular path and reaches there, that's an intelligent person, isn't it? So right now, every human being is aspiring to be joyful, so if one person is joyful by his own nature, definitely he must be intelligent.

Maybe socially, somebody may think he's a fool, but the real fool who thinks that a joyful person is a fool doesn't know what he's missing. Somebody may be so joyful that he doesn't care to build a business for himself, make money, or have fine clothes or this or that. So someone else who's wearing good clothes and has lots of money may think this person is a fool. He thinks, "He's just happy, he's just joyful by his own nature. In rags, on the street he's joyful, what a fool!" But see who the fool really is.

With great difficulty you gather all these things because you want to be joyful but you're not joyful, so aren't you a fool? Somebody who without doing anything is simply joyful by his own nature, is he a fool? Who is intelligent? The man who fulfills the purpose for which he is doing what he is doing is an intelligent person. So, socially, how you judge him doesn't matter, existentially a joyful person is obviously an intelligent person.

Miserable people have passed off as intelligent people in the world, because they have miserable questions and complications in their minds. Unfortunately, this unnecessary complexity which creates misery and burden upon themselves, has been glorified as intelligence. Just unbridled intellectual activity is considered as intelligence but it is not. True intelligence is when you're absolutely thoughtless and fully alert. Intelligence then functions in a completely different way.

> *Just unbridled intellectual activity is considered as intelligence but it is not. True intelligence is when you're absolutely thoughtless and fully alert. Intelligence then functions in a completely different way.*

Why no Joy?

Push start and self-start

Dev and Lila were walking quietly on the beach enjoying the evening breeze.

Dev looked at the rise and fall of the waves and told Lila how amazing it was, as if the waves had a life of their own.

Lila was in a funny mood and she quickly remarked, "Your mood is quite like that Dev, it just goes up and down, up and down...! If only you told me Dev where your mood regulator is, I could then have had some fun with your moods...!"

Dev did not want to have a discussion on such advanced technologies.

Sadhguru: Whenever you experience a certain amount of Joy, it always blossoms from within and finds an external expression. It never rains upon you. So definitely it is from within. It is just that you have kept the starter button outside.

If the Sun is up there, you can't be joyous because it has to set. The Sun must set for you to be happy. For 12 hours he is up there, but that's not good enough. Those few moments when he is rising and setting are the only moments you can be joyful. This is what you have done to your life also. When he is up there, you curse him, you cannot be joyful.

See, the very way you are leading your life, you're making it a no-win possibility. How many times in the day can the Sun set? Only once. The moment you say 'Oh I am so happy and joyful when I see the sunset' you have made it very clear that for only a few moments in a day, you can be happy; and tomorrow if it is cloudy, even those few moments are not possible. And here, sitting at the foothills of the mountain, you can never be happy because you can't see the sunset.

So this induction from the outside is not a necessity but it is a compulsive state that you have gotten into.

For example, you may not be old enough for this, but if you bought a car in the 1940s, along with the car you had to get yourself two servants, because in the morning you would need a 'push start'. In the 1950s if you got a car, one servant would do, because it became 'crank start'.

Today all your cars are 'self-start', aren't they? Is it not time that you put a 'self-start' on your Joy? I am talking about upgrading technologies. (Laughs) Is it not time?

The very way you are making your life, you're making it a no-win possibility. .... It is just that you have kept the starter button outside.

Inner happiness and external Joy

"Where are you going this early ?" Lila asked Dev who was rushing out at 6 am on a Sunday morning which was unusual for him.

"I don't really know..."replied Dev

"If you don't know where you want to go my dear, how will you GET THERE?" Lila stumped him with her remark.

"Oh Lila, I am just trying to go out and get some peace of mind..."

"Why do you have to go out for that?" Lila exclaimed.

Sadhguru: Is there any human being who has never known a moment of Joy in his life? It is not possible at all, even the most miserable man in the world has known Joy. It is not that he is not capable of Joy. Just as he is capable of misery he is also capable of Joy.

Right now his only problem is that he is not able to hold it. In fact he is very miserable because he has lost his Joy. Isn't it? One of the reasons why people are doubly miserable is, 'Oh, yesterday how wonderful it was and today what has happened to my life?' That doubles and multiplies their misery, isn't it? So every human being essentially has known Joy, at least for one moment in his life.

So, if you are capable of making yourself joyful for one moment – I say 'making yourself' because you are either making yourself miserable or joyful – you are capable of making yourself joyful all the time. The seat of your experience is within you, not outside of you. This is the fundamental shift in understanding that is needed for you to be joyful.

People ask, how to get inner happiness? I ask them, have you ever known external Joy? Maybe by consuming alcohol you felt joyful, and you thought that the Joy is external, isn't it? Joy always happens internally, no matter what you do. Always within you, isn't it? Never outside of you.

Right now, one of the main reasons why you have become miserable is, instead of falling back into your Joy, you are trying to pursue Joy. Not understanding that the seat of experience is within you, you are trying to put all your energies out towards something as if Joy is hanging out there.

The reason why you are unhappy is that you are trying to go away from yourself which is the basis of Joy. You are trying to find it somewhere on the street. The very fact that you are trying to go away creates misery because the Joy is here, but you are going somewhere else. You are going away from it.

So, you are capable of Joy. The only thing is you have managed to create it for just a few moments, for the rest of the time you are creating many moments of misery.

If you are capable of creating one moment the way you want it, are you not capable of creating one more moment the way you want it? One more and one more and one more? After all the whole life is just that, it is one moment at a time, fortunately. Moments are not coming and battering you in bunches, they are coming only one at a time. If you just know how to be joyful in this moment, you are joyful for eternity. If you do not know how, then you are lost forever.

One of the main reasons why you have become miserable is, instead of falling back into your Joy, you are trying to pursue Joy.

Crowds have always been stupid

"This remote control for the television does not seem to work Dad" screamed an impatient Arya.

"I have a clever idea son, if this television is not working, why don't you go out and watch the garden instead, it is so beautiful and it doesn't even need a remote control," Dev said teasingly.

"But Dad kids love to watch television not the garden." exclaimed Arya now losing his patience.

"Well my son, just imagine, if from tomorrow all the kids start watching the garden, then is that what you will do too?" Dev tried to reason with his son.

Sadhguru: You don't know what sanity is, because you have an insane mind. Where there is sanity, there will be Joy. Only an insane mind creates what it doesn't want. If you had a sane mind, would it create what you don't want? Insanity means you have no control over your mind, your mind does not do what you want it to do, it does its own ridiculous things. So just because a large percentage of the population has joined you, it doesn't make you right. Crowds have always been stupid.

Now you may think that it is all about controlling the mind. I'm not talking about control. If you allow the natural process within you to happen without you messing it, Joy is the only way to be. Now, your physical body is an instrument that is useful to you only if it functions the way you want it to. Otherwise this is not a good body, isn't it? Similarly the mind, if right now I want to be joyful, it should allow me to be joyful. When I want to be joyful, if it makes me miserable, when I want to be resolute if it makes me shaky, then this is a ridiculous mind, this is a useless mind.

The question is not about control, the question is are you and do you have a working mind at all? If you have a car that doesn't go where you want to go, would you call it a car? If you have a car whose wheels are locked up, do you call it a vehicle to travel in? So you have a mind that doesn't take instructions from you, it doesn't create what you want, it creates some other nonsense that you don't want. Such minds should have been kept in an asylum, because there are too many of them let loose.

Only an insane mind creates what it doesn't want. If you had a sane mind, would it create what you don't want?

Two large heaps

Lila was admiring herself in front of the mirror when Dev stepped into the room.

"Stop admiring yourself like this Lila" said Dev.

"Am I not looking wonderful Dev?" Lila said posing again in front of the mirror.

"Well, actually ...that mirror has just been polished a couple of days back you know...that's why probably...you know... it is not because of you!" Dev smiled looking at Lila who did not like this tongue-in-cheek comment.

Sadhguru: See, only the being in you can be joyful; but right now no such thing as you actually exists. What you are is just a huge heap of garbage that you gathered from social circumstances.

Please look into yourself and see what is it here within you that you can call as myself? It is just a hodge-podge of stuff that you've gathered from the books that you read, from the people who live around you and from the things that are around you. Just a huge heap of impressions that you have taken in. There's no 'you' there.

Actually, there are two huge heaps; one is the body and the other is the mind. Your physical body is just a heap of food that you've eaten isn't it? Just see how huge this heap has become from the time that you were born till now? (Laughs) Your mind is just a heap of impressions that you've taken in. In these two large heaps, where are you? You don't even exist so how can you be joyful? There's no such possibility.

First you must have an existence and then being joyful arises. Right now, you're just a reflection of the society in which you live, there's no such thing as you in this. Only an individual can know Joy.

Right now you're a crowd, you're an assembly of people, isn't it? This assembly will not know Joy, because this assembly is a huge mess of contradictions and confrontations within you. No war needs to happen on this planet, human beings are fighting battles within themselves endlessly, isn't it? You don't need guns and swords to fight battles — you can just sit with your eyes closed and start a battle of your own.

Right now, you're just a reflection of the society in which you live, there's no such thing as you in this. Only an individual can know Joy.

Handle at the wrong end

Dev and Arya were busy playing with a bat and a ball. Dev was new to this game and Arya had already played this for several months with his friends in their backyard.

Each time Dev tried to hit the ball hard he could not hit it far. After the third attempt he was quiet frustrated. "I just can't hit the ball..."

"That is because you are holding the bat at the wrong end Dad!" laughed Arya heartily.

Sadhguru: The reason why Joy is not a constant factor in your life is because you're trying to handle it from the wrong end.

If you want to grow a tree, you have to plant and nurture that little seed first, isn't it? If you are painting a tree, you could start from the top end, but if you want a real tree you cannot start from the top end, isn't it?

Let us say you like mangoes but you don't care much for the other parts of the tree. So in your garden, you first want to create mangoes and then the tree. It doesn't work like that. You can buy mangoes without a tree in the market. You can bring a dozen mangoes home, but you cannot grow it in your garden. If season after season, you want mangoes dropping on your head, you can't have it if you try growing the tree from the top end. It grows only from the bottom end.

You want the very way of your being to be joyful, not receive Joy as a prize that you get at the end of misery – one long miserable year, and you get Joy as a prize one day. No. You're not looking at life that way, you want Joy to be a constant factor, you want it to be your quality and you want it to be your way of being.

If that is so, you have to understand how it grows, not from the other end. From the other end, once in a way you can buy it in the market, but it doesn't last, it keeps crashing. And that's the issue, isn't it?

You want the very way of your being to be joyful, not receive Joy as a prize that you get at the end of misery.

The reason why Joy is not a constant factor in your life is because you're trying to handle it from the wrong end.

Return on investment

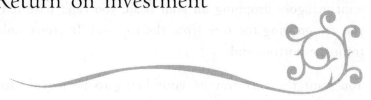

Arya did not like losing when he played games with his father. Dev was aware of this fact and he too wanted to see his son win.

Then one day Dev hit upon a big idea. He created a game with a pack of cards and a set of totally unique rules.

The loser of the game was the one with the most number of cards. The winner had lesser cards. Thus whenever Arya had more cards, even though that meant a defeat, in Arya's mind he was the winner.

So the clever ploy was that if Arya won the game, Dev would say he had won. If the kid lost the game then Dev would let him count the number of cards and make him believe he was the lucky winner and that he, Dev, was the unlucky loser.

This ruse worked quite well. Dev and Arya began enjoying this arrangement.

Sadhguru: When you work hard and have all the money in the world, you always dream of going on a vacation or sleeping on the beach, or trekking in the wild, or not having a care in the world, not having to get up and go to office the next morning.

Let us say tomorrow your business burns down. Oh! That is the opportunity to sleep on the beach, walk in the forest, not have a care in the world; but you don't make a profit out of it, you make a loss out of everything.

Now when you came here into this world, you came without a single investment, isn't it? So whatever the hell happens with your life, anyway you're in profit, aren't you? Whatever happens, you can't lose.

This life is made in such a way that you just can't lose. Whichever way life happens, you're still on the profit side, never in loss. But all the time, you cry about your profits.

If you're not married, you cry 'oh, no marriage in my life.' Can you see how happy all the married people are? When you get married, you know, you always marry the wrong man or the wrong woman. Always. That is because there is no right man or right woman in the world. And now if something happens and if it breaks up, then you cry 'it is broken.'

Please see, you have learnt to cry about everything. When the Sun comes up, and it is too hot, you cry. When the Sun sets, it is too dark, you cry. Winter is too cold, you cry, summer is too hot, you cry. The way you're going at it, I think the only place you will be all right is in your grave. You'll not be all right with life obviously because you are against the very natural phenomena of life.

You have taken such an attitude in your mind that you don't want the very simple happenings of life — birth, death and happenings in life. Your demanding life should not happen.

Now when you came here into this world, you came without a single investment, isn't it? So whatever the hell happens with your life, anyway you're on profit, aren't you?

My misery, my way !

Dev and Lila met a few friends at the fancy dress party that Friday evening at a neighbour's home. Most of the people could not recognize each other.

For a moment Lila felt that everyone was looking so happy because each one was not able to recognize the other and enjoyed the fact that they were hiding their own face too!

Sadhguru: You're not in terms with the fundamental reality; you have fancy ideas about life in your head. You have no perception of life or life-sense in you, simply ego-sense. All the time, your one and only problem and the very basis of your misery is that life is not happening the way you think it should be happening. Isn't this the only reason why you're miserable?

Being the kind of mess that you are, if everything happens the way you think it should, do you think you could live here? Do you know what a mess you would make out of this world?

If everything happens the way you and everybody else wants it to happen, can you imagine how it would be? The world will be destroyed in no time! Fortunately, it is not happening your way.

And if everything happens your way where will I go? Where will everybody else go? Then each one of us will need to have our own worlds, and that's what you have done right now. Though you live in the same house, please see, you live in a world of your own and your family lives in its own world.

Since you could not handle reality, you have chosen hallucination. When you go on hallucinatory trips, you can sometimes have good trips or bad trips, but you have no control over your hallucinations.

You can guide them a little bit, but the very nature of hallucination is such that you really have no control. If you have control over it, it just becomes conscious thinking. You can't float around in your conscious thinking, you're always grounded in conscious thinking.

All the time, your one and only problem and the very basis of your misery is life is not happening the way you think it should happen.

100 % Idealistic idiots

Dev cursed the unforeseen rainy weather when he stepped out to take a walk. He ran inside and quickly picked up a large umbrella, put on his raincoat and then stepped out again within a few minutes. As luck would have it, the rains had stopped and it was shining bright outside.

This was not the weather forecast at all. How come it rained? Dev picked up a couple of newspapers to check the weather reports. Each forecast was very different but none spoke of the rains.

He did not know whether to trust the newspaper, his umbrella, his raincoat or his instinct. He definitely did not trust his mood right now.

Sadhguru: Anything that happens is just a reflection of the outside. For example, on Holi* everybody is merry and throwing colours at each other. You too can be happy, but if you are going for an interview and they spray you with colour, you're going to be bitterly miserable. So it doesn't matter what it is, it'll depend on how you reflect it within yourself.

---

* Indian festival of colours

So if you depend on the outside to bring Joy to you, you need to understand that the outside never happens 100% the way you want it, it happens the way you want it only to some extent.

Those idealistic idiots who think of an ideal situation are not in terms with external reality. That is the problem they have. You should know, not one person in this world will happen exactly the way you want him to happen – not your husband, wife, parents, children, friends – nobody. Not even your dog will be exactly the way you want him to be, he will do something else. So when this is the reality, at least this one person, you, must happen the way you want yourself to be, isn't it?

So if you did happen the way you want yourself to be, what would be your natural choice, Joy or misery? Joy is the natural choice, isn't it? You don't need any teaching on that; you don't need anybody's advice on that. You don't need the help of scriptures to make this choice.

The very natural choice is Joy because that's your original nature, that's not something that you have to desire. That's not something that you have to pursue, that is not something that you have to attain. If you fall back into your original nature, joyfulness is the only way you will be.

> Not even your dog will be exactly the way you want him to be, he will do something else. So when this is the reality, at least this one person, you, must happen the way you want yourself to be, isn't it?

Whodunnit?

There was this huge pile of trash outside Arya's classroom and the teacher was rather annoyed. She looked at the first kid standing around and she asked him "Who did this?" The kid quickly said "Somebody else, ma'am". She asked a second kid and he was equally quick to say "Somebody else ma'am"....It was Arya's turn and Arya replied on being asked "Somebody else ma'am".

The teacher was keen on knowing who this person named 'somebody else' was.

Sadhguru: Once you hold somebody else as the source of who or what you are right now, that person will invariably fail you in so many different ways.

We have already looked at this – no human being is going to function 100% the way you want him to. The bigger your expectations, the more failure you will experience with people around you. So when they fail you and things do not happen, or they do not happen the way you think they should happen, and you truly believe they are the cause for your misery then naturally anger will set in.

Once anger sets in and gets organized, it becomes hate. When hate takes action, it becomes murder. So from the very moment you think that the source of who you are or the basis of your experience in this life is somebody else, you have started the game.

Maybe initially it started in a pleasant way. 'Oh, I am so happy because of you.' Now, this game is going to turn sour in no time because that same person who did certain things and made you happy is going to do certain things tomorrow that he or she wants, which is going to make you very unhappy, because no human being can live up to your expectations. Nobody.

Not one human being on this planet will behave exactly the way you expect him to behave. So once this happens, you think somebody else is the source of your misery. When you believe that somebody else is the source of your pain and suffering, naturally anger and hatred will follow.

> *The very moment you think that the source of who you are or the basis of your experience in this life is somebody else, you have started the game.*

The greed for greed

Dev had a friend whom he spent a lot of time with. The friend believed that he was a content and peaceful person and not greedy at all. Dev agreed with him because he found his friend very peaceful and never clamouring for anything more.

One day he mustered some courage and asked his friend this nagging doubt he had about his greed. His friend gave a hearty laugh but was not too sure whether Dev was saying the right thing or not. Then the friend quickly added, "What is wrong in being greedy to be content?"

Sadhguru: Greed is a very relative term. One person thinks living in a palace is a necessity. Another person thinks it is greed.

You know, this happened sometime ago. I met a swami who lived under a tree and made it his life's mission to constantly deride all those other swamis who had built some shelter for themselves. He spent his life constantly saying how these people were lost, corrupted and had given themselves to comfort and luxury while he lived under the simple shelter of a tree, braving all the rigors of nature.

He said 'they are pompous, look at the way they have decorated their huts.' All that had been done to beautify their huts was a flower garden had been laid and the huts painted a little bit. The swami thought all this was pompous. I had to remind him, that thinking that he was better than everybody else was the most pompous, stupid thing that anyone could do.

So greed is very relative. In your perception, you are never greedy. Somebody else who has reached a place where you aspire to get is greedy. You may try to make a million bucks and don't make it, but the man who makes it is greedy in your eyes. If you make it, one million bucks is not greedy, 10 million is greedy because somebody else has got there.

The reason why this need to accumulate is so strong is because there is a certain sense of insufficiency. Who you are, is not enough. You want to be something more than what you are right now. The moment you reach there, you want to be something more; little more, little more, little more ... it goes on.

I want you to know this, even if we make you the king or queen of this planet – don't worry, I have no intention of making such a mistake – you won't stop there, you will still look up at the stars because there is something within you that is constantly seeking boundless expansion.

It is not going to settle how ever much you give to it. You give it the whole galaxy; it will still look for more galaxies. So you are greedy, as you know it in the world today because your inner nature wants to find boundless expansion, but you're trying to satisfy this thirst for boundlessness through physical means.

Nothing wrong with your greed; your greed is actually a spiritual process. It is just that you have not given it proper expression. It is like you want to go to the infinite, so you start counting 1, 2, 3, 4, 5... It will just become endless counting; you will never know the infinite.

It is just like your want to go to the moon by riding a bullock cart. You think that by flogging the bulls you will get there. No, you may kill the bulls, but you will not get there. If you want to get there you need the right kind of vehicle.

Something within you is longing for boundlessness. If this longing has to be fulfilled, it definitely cannot be done through physical means.

Nothing wrong with your greed; your greed is actually a spiritual process. It is just that you have not given it proper expression.

The depth of idiots

Lila was learning to drive the car with Dev's help on weekends. She had learnt to drive a few years ago but wanted to freshen up her practice. Each time she would go over a bump on the road, she would learn to steer the wheel a little better. On straight flat roads, Lila would not drive too well. Dev wanted her to improve on steering the car a little better and quicker, but Lila was not responding well to the training.

"Lila, Lila you seem to turn the car better only after we go through a bump or a pot-hole? Why don't you steer well when the road is quite OKAY? I just cannot understand….." shouted an impatient, tired Dev.

Sadhguru: Most human beings learn and look deeper only when they are in pain and that's not a sign of intelligence. When people are joyful, they must look at life with great depth; but when they are happy, they live frivolously. Something has to go dead wrong in their life for them to look deeper.

If you tell somebody you are staying in an ashram, they will ask you 'Oh, what happened, did your husband die? Did your child die? Did some other terrible tragedy befall you?'. People ask these questions because most of the time

they only seek the deeper dimensions of life when
something terrible happens, something or everything goes
dead wrong with their life. That has been the unfortunate
history of humanity, but it need not be so. Just because a
large number of people do something, it does not mean
that is the right thing to do.

If you look back, probably in the '70s almost 80% of the
men smoked. Yes? That was the right thing to do. Without
smoking, you were not man enough, isn't it? Isn't that the
image that was created? The Marlboro man, you know he
was a real man. A man without a cigarette in his hand was
not a real man. So that's an image we created and we
believed and younger generations took to it even earlier,
but now there is a huge campaign that proclaims that
smoking is some kind of devil's nonsense.

The campaign is so strong in the world, today you can see
that the number of people smoking has dropped so
dramatically. I will tell you, if the campaign continues like
this, in 50 years time probably nobody will smoke. Then
people will find it hard to believe that in the past, people
smoked a lot, coughed a lot and even got cancer and yet
continued to smoke.

They won't understand why people in the past did such a
thing. When we are even attempting to reduce smoking
automobiles, why would people smoke? Two generations
later, they won't believe smoking existed.

This existed to such an extent that during the Victorian
age, in England and in Europe, it was actually fashionable
to have tuberculosis. Did you know this? Really. It was
fashion to have tuberculosis. Many young intellectuals,

poets, and artists died because they refused to get treated since being an intellectual meant that they had to keep coughing. The understanding was that if you looked healthy and robust you had no mind, you were just brawn, no brain.

One of the greatest poets that we lost to tuberculosis was John Keats who died at the age of 25 because he refused to get his tuberculosis treated. Can you believe that now? This was just, a century or two ago. That's how it is. Your intelligence is so deeply entangled with the social identification that you have taken on, your brains are not working in line with the life within you.

So you need to understand, your intelligence is deeply entangled with the identifications that you take on in your life. The source of misery is just this; your mind, your body, your emotion is working against the fundamental life force within you. The life force within you is always longing to become an exuberant joyfulness, but your mind and emotion and even your body sometimes are going in anti-directions.

That sounds stupid, isn't it? Stupid in a much deeper way than you would ever understand it. Stupid people won't understand how deeply stupid they are. It is a very deep sense of stupidity because you are working against your own life.

Your intelligence is so deeply entangled with the social identification that you have taken on, your brains are not working in line with the life within you; it is working against your own life. That is the source of misery.

Thousand impressions

Arya just loved what he was doing at the beach. Each time he went into the water and pushed his feet hard on the moist sand, they made a deep impression on the sand. Then he waited for the sea to hit the sand in its flow and just wash away those impressions and be smooth again.

This was a wonderful discovery for him. The sea was just tirelessly wiping out the impressions on the shore without any effort at all.

Sadhguru: As a child you were joyful. You were, there is no question about it. Even when you were a child, certain things, impressions, activities, atmospheres could just suppress you. There is a certain sense of helplessness, even though children are by nature bubbling with life energy that is joyful.

They are also more susceptible to other people's will, than you are right now as an adult. A physically ill child, unable to bear the pain, unable to bear the suffering, may make himself sad, that's different. But, there are many healthy children, who are sad. This is happening not because it is the child's nature but because the early imprints in life are such. So the kind of over-bearing atmosphere that people create around you will accordingly leave an imprint on you.

There are also other kinds of imprints within the human being which could make him sad. It may be just pushing that person to realize this is not it, but irrespective of whether external situations or inner imprints are pushing you, you still have a choice.

If you are conscious enough, you have a choice to be beyond these imprints and still be joyful because all your impressions come from outside, but not your Joy. Impressions can come, impressions can go, but Joy does not come and go. It is the life source within you.

The only thing is whether you allow it to find expression or not. When I say there is no joyless person in the world, maybe there are joyless faces in the world, joyless bodies, joyless minds, but there are no joyless beings in the world. Every being is a joyful being.

If you get entangled in the process of your body, entangled in the process of your mind, entangled in the process of your emotion, there are million reasons and ways to make yourself joyless or miserable right now. You can be joyless by just thinking about something, remembering something that was unpleasant, or even by creating something that may be unpleasant tomorrow.

People are doing this all the time, isn't it? Right now, nobody needs to poke you with a knife for you to be miserable. Something that somebody said 10 years ago can still make you miserable. Your fear that somebody may say something tomorrow is already making you miserable. Or if somebody did not say something that they were supposed to say, that is making you miserable too.

There are endless ways to make you miserable. It is madness, that's all. Whether you have been miserable as a child, or an adult is not the point. I don't see any adults in the world. Small-bodied children, big-bodied children, that's all I see.

> *Impressions can come, impressions can go, but Joy does not come and go. It is the life source within you.*

Ignorance is bliss

Dev was very upset at the television as it was just not working well for a couple of days and he did not know what to do. He finally went and gave the TV set a little tap on the right side but there was no change. Then he gave a hard tap on the left side but could not see any improvement. Then he slapped it hard on the top and still there was no real change. Finally he went behind the TV set and banged it hard with his fist after which he heard a small sound of something bursting inside.

Now he knew that this method of repairing the television set would not really work.

Sadhguru: You've always been told that ignorance is bliss. Till life takes a bite at you, yes, it is blissful. See, right now, if you go up a tall building and jump off from there, do you know how joyful it will be? Just that free fall? But that's only till you hit the ground. Once you hit terra firma, then you're a smear, no more Joy.

Suppose there was no consequence of hitting the ground, I'm sure every human being would be climbing up the tallest building and jumping off again and again because it is such a Joy. Why do you think people take roller coaster rides? Why do you think they're bungee jumping? Why do you think they're skydiving? Only because jumping without the consequence of smashing into the earth is very joyful.

So if you just walk off a tall building, it is very joyful, because ignorance is bliss. But only for those few seconds till you hit the ground. So idiots can be joyful, only till life gets them, and life usually gets them. If life doesn't, death will.

Now, I'm not talking about that kind of Joy that is subject to the process of life and death. I'm talking about that dimension of Joy that is neither subject to the process of life, nor the process of death.

> *Idiots can be joyful, only till life gets them, and life usually gets them. If life doesn't, death will.*

Pride and prejudice

Dev often found Lila behaving as if she was part of a Boy's Scouts Camp. When she was gossiping with her neighbours she would behave as though their group was the one that was responsible for running this neighbourhood. When she was with her friends she would behave as funnily as most of them would during those couple of hours. When she would go to the school to drop Arya, her chatter with the other mothers was a different tone. To him it looked like she was so proud to be part of that particular group in each case.

His only lament was that she had no pride in being a part of the couple that he and she were.

Sadhguru: Thinking too much of yourself and all the fancy ideas that you have about yourself is pride. When you're not in touch with reality, that's pride.

People have always been telling you that you must have pride in what you do. These are all like sergeants giving soldier talk. Do you know what's a soldier talk? Just before the soldiers go to the battle you know what kind of talk the sergeants give? "Oh come on, let's go and get those sons-of-bitches, those cowards, they're no good nonsense, we're going to just go and maul them, we're going to shoot them to death." This is the soldier talk. The sergeants know it is not true, but the soldier believes it is true. That gives him the confidence to go and brave risky situations.

If this sergeant sits there and tells the soldiers the reality, 'See when you're going there, you're walking into bullets and cannons, okay? All of you may be just blown to bits before you even put your finger on the trigger', they won't go. He's has to make the other group utterly useless, 'filthy nonsense, we're going to trample over them with our boots, we don't need guns to beat those guys' – this creates a sense of pride.

'Who are we? We're Indians. What are we? We're the strongest people in the world. Who are we? We're Americans, we are the biggest nation, the strongest nation, we can just walk, without boots we can walk through the world, we don't need anything'. This kind of talk gives the soldier pride with his identity of being something and to just go and do something during war. This is one way of initiating action.

When you have too many idiots around you, you have to build a sense of pride in them, otherwise you can't get anything out of them. If you evolve within, no pride is needed to perform action; you can perform action out of pure sense, absolute sense.

When there's no pride, there's no prejudice, because pride and prejudice are not different. The moment you have pride in something, you are prejudiced against something else, isn't it? When you say 'I'm a proud Indian', naturally you're prejudiced against something else that is not Indian.

So, pride is definitely rooted in a certain prejudice and this prejudice is needed to goad the stupid into action. Without it, you can't get them into action.

Just because lots of people are stupid, can you just wait till all of them get enlightened to do something? No, that would also be stupid. So you've got to make the donkeys also work. A donkey is stupid, alright? But is it useless? Similarly, when I say you're stupid, I'm not saying you're useless.

If you evolve within, no pride is needed to perform action; you can perform action out of pure sense, absolute sense.

Non-stop bus ride

Arya came to Dev one Saturday evening with a bag full of toys. He was dragging the bag with all his strength since it was very large for his size. Dev looked a little puzzled.

Arya put the bag in front of him and said "Dad...I am just not able to count the number of toys in this bag...How do I know how many toys there are in this bag and in the cupboard?"

Dev had no desire to sit and count all his hundreds of toys. So he gave him a cryptic reply "Son, just count the number of times you smile in a day and that is usually equal to the number of toys you have..."

Arya's little mind knew to some extent there was a link between a smile and a toy but did not know to what extent.

Sadhguru: The basis of your experience is you. It is so. Destiny is a word that we coined to refer to all those things that we created unconsciously. Destiny is not falling upon you from somewhere and it is not written by someone else. Destiny is just the sum result of all your actions and impressions that you've taken in.

You have taken in any number of impressions. This

complex amalgamation of impressions that you have received through your five senses, slowly over a period of time, take on a certain tendency. This tendency tends to push you in a particular direction.

So in between, if you want to go a certain way, it doesn't let you, it just keeps taking you some other way. It is just like your getting into a bus and something interesting is happening on the way. You want to stick your neck out but the bus keeps going. Now you look helpless as you actually want to go and see the show there but the bus is just taking you away from the show. Now you make yourself miserable, you cry and yell, not understanding that it is you who got into the bus.

Probably you would understand it better in terms of floating on a river. The river is just taking you on because it has a certain tendency to find its way. So according to its tendency it is going but these tendencies were not created by you but the accumulations that created this tendency are you.

Because you gathered all this in total unconsciousness, it all looks like something is falling upon you from somewhere. Because the very nature of your existence and experience here is anything that you're not conscious of, anything that you're not aware of does not exist for you.

It doesn't matter how big a force it is, right now while you're sitting here, you're not aware of the huge mountain. When you are not aware of the mountain, the mountain does not exist for you.

Destiny is just the sum result of all your actions and impressions that you've taken in.

100 % Ego

Lila was very annoyed with Arya's poor and illegible handwriting. Each time she would look at his notes and be most frustrated and say

"Arya why is your writing so poor?"

Arya would smile and give his clever reply "This is not my writing Mom, it's just this stupid slippery pencil trying to slip out of my hand onto this slippery notebook..."

Sadhguru: When you call the nasty part of you the ego, you're blaming it on somebody. You talk about ego as if it is another identity in you but it is not. It is not your ego; it is you who is turning nasty. You were turning nasty pretty often but now you're seldom turning nasty.

Why your nastiness has dropped is because you were thinking about so many things that were happening in your life, and you knew it is all because of this, this, this, this and this. You either dropped all those things or they went away, whichever way. Now, you're beginning to understand that you are the reason but you have not gotten there 100%. This moment if you see 100% that 'everything that is me is me, not my ego, not my parents, not my culture, not my influence, not my this or that, it is me, me and me alone', your nastiness will cease.

If you are unable to experience this, you have to understand who is not letting you experience it. You have to make that sink deep into you that you are the source of your misery, you are the source of your Joy, nobody else, nobody else at all, nothing else at all but you.

If you understand this, suddenly, experientially if you understand this, you will find there can be no nastiness at all. There cannot be, because your intelligence will not allow you to turn yourself nasty for any reason, because you know it is you. If you think it is somebody else, immediately you can become nasty, isn't it?

Don't keep ascribing your nastiness to other more complex identities, like ego. No, it is just you; it is you who's sometimes capable of turning pleasant, sometimes capable of turning unpleasant. It is you all the way.

> *Whenever you get nasty, you don't want to see that it is you who's being nasty, you say it is my ego. It is not your ego; it is you who are turning nasty.*

Thought expressway

Dev, Lila and Arya were on a drive along the countryside and had lost their way while trying to reach a beautiful garden in that part of the countryside.

Dev finally asked a farmer "Does this road go to the special flower garden Sir?"

The farmer looked around and then looked at Dev in the eye, smiled and said "Well the road does not go anywhere sir, you need to go there...."

Sadhguru: A thought doesn't take you anywhere. A thought just makes suggestions, taking it or not taking is up to you. Thoughts are not yours; they are the social impact or an input. So they are like suggestions coming up, whether you take them on, or you just ignore them, the choice is still yours, isn't it?

A thought never does anything; it only keeps coming and going. Which one do you want to pick? To retain the choice as to which one you want to pick is what is needed right now. Right now you have no choice, you pick up everything that comes up. So that's a mess.

> *A thought doesn't take you anywhere. A thought just makes*
> *suggestions, taking it or not taking is up to you.*

The path of Joy

Fix your accounts

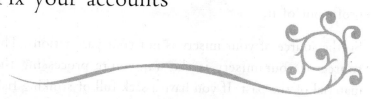

Lila knew a bunch of men and women in the neighbourhood who were an interesting lot. They could conjure stories from a situation and gossip.

Recently an old man in the neighbourhood, was hospitalized. The gossip-mongers had a suspicion that the man was sick because of the severe mental harassment caused by his argumentative daughter-in-law.

They created a complete sequence of stories and statements, which made the old man, seem truly harassed by this gladiator of a daughter-in-law. Each story was more interesting and imaginative than the previous one and so vivid as if they had actually seen it happen!

Sadhguru: Who's retributing you? Is somebody keeping accounts? Only you are keeping accounts and after all, when there is no audit, you could fix your accounts a little bit, isn't it?

Whatever nonsense happens with your life, you can make it into a great profit if you want, because after all you handle the balance sheet. There's no review from anywhere. So depending on whatever has happened, you can show as loss, the things that are your sob stories in your balance sheets. Otherwise, whatever is happening, you can make a profit out of it.

So the source of your misery is not your past actions. The source of your misery is the way you're processing the material of the past. If you have a sack full of stinking fish in your bag, you can make good manure out of it, or you can sleep with this sack and be terribly miserable.

Especially if you have a very filthy past, you can make a great wonderful garden out of it, because it makes good manure, filth makes good manure. Or you can smear yourself with it and feel terrible about it. So it is not the sack full of nonsense that you've gathered which is making you miserable, it is the way you're handling it right now.

The source of your misery is not your past actions. The source of your misery is the way you're processing the material of the past.

Going out to get Joy

A young man who lived down the street from where Dev and Lila stayed would stand by the park in the evening and eagerly wait to help older people cross the road at the pedestrian crossing.

One evening when Dev was taking a walk, he noticed that the young man was not looking very happy.

The young man looked at him and offered to help him cross the road. Dev found this a little strange. The young man insisted. Dev felt very awkward. He had to find the reason for this.

On persuading, the young man said, "I am so used to doing this each evening that one day when it does not happen, I don't feel very good... so please let me help you today..."

Sadhguru: You cannot get Joy. You are either joyful or you are not, that's all. It is just that you have enslaved yourself to a certain type of action, which you believe, will stimulate Joy in you. So now if you want to be joyful, many other people in the world should not have what they need. Isn't it? That's why we have kept the country the way we have, because we believe we must help everybody. If you want to help everybody, there must be a lot of needy people, isn't it?

Suppose everybody is doing well, then whom will you help and how will you be joyful? Maybe that's why affluent societies are becoming miserable because they cannot help anybody since everybody is doing fine. So, just see what kind of self-defeating postures you are taking in your life, in the name of goodness, in the name of passion, in the name of great values.

Now if you want to be happy, you need to feed the hungry. That means there must always be hungry people in the world. Suppose there is a situation tomorrow where everybody is well-fed, then you will not be joyful anymore. So, somewhere unknowingly you will go about constantly working towards creating a situation where lots of people can never eat properly. And this is happening.

Human beings are consciously doing this. Right now there is more food than what the 6 or 7 billion people who are on this planet can eat. We actually have enough food to feed approximately 18 to 20 billion people on the planet, but still 50% of the people don't eat well.

They cannot eat well simply because people who have food are sitting on the food. They cannot eat any more but they are sitting on the food. They won't let other people eat but once in a way they want to give aid. Once in a way they want to do some charity and buy a ticket to heaven or whatever nonsense they have in their heads.

Human beings are ensuring that a large number of people don't live well because they have all crooked, twisted ideas within themselves.

Why should your Joy be linked to somebody else's
helplessness? Only if somebody is helpless he needs help,
isn't it? If everybody is doing well, does it mean you can't
be joyful? But that's the kind of position you are taking
within yourself.

You need to understand that if you see a miserable world,
that's the nature of human mind. If you see a joyful world,
that's the nature of the minds which exist there, because
the world around you is just a larger manifestation of
whatever kind of mind you carry.

*You cannot get Joy. You are either joyful or you are not, that's
all.*

Shades of grey

Dev was often scared at the breakfast table when he found Lila happy and whistling. Whenever she was in such a delightful mood, she would just mix up the breakfast dishes. He would find some sugar on his toast, salt in his tea and she would have heated the apples. Lila would be too delighted to be bothered.

Sadhguru: If everybody in the office or work place is joyful what'll the dynamics be? One thing that will happen is that everybody will do their best.

Of course any work needs to be organized at least to some extent. Whether people are joyful or miserable, work has to be done the way it has to be done. Now if I am very joyful and I walk on my head and go into the office, it won't work like that. You have to conduct different work aspects, as it should be done, according to the requirement.

There are many aspects to organizing work and however you may organize it, in any work situation where 100, 200 or 1000 people work, there will be any number of shortcomings. There will be any number of areas that are grey areas into which somebody else steps in.

It is always like this; there is no clear-cut organization anywhere in the world. If you do such a thing, no work will happen. Somewhere there must be a meeting place for the work to progress, but those meeting places are the problem places for people. Now people are in conflict because they have to tread the same path at the same time. If two joyous people got the opportunity to do something together, how would the situation be?

All those so-called grey areas which are right now problematic areas would be a great sense of coming together and producing something wonderful, isn't it? Right now, those patches of work where people have to meet and mingle and do something together are the areas of trouble. They do their own work individually.

There are points where your work has to merge with somebody elses and then go forward, that's where the problem is. Isn't it? If there is a problem with the work itself, that's different. I am talking about the human element of the problem that is the major problem.

In any office, in any work place, the real issues of work are one thing, but the human issues are big. The real issues could be handled pretty easily if all these human beings were one cohesive force, but to make them into one cohesive force is very, very difficult when they don't know what Joy is.

If you are a joyous person on a certain day, do you see how flexible you are? Have you noticed this? How flexible you are in your attitudes, how willing to bend you are? You are willing to become a doormat for somebody, because you are happy anyway, but on a day when you are unhappy do you know the kind of demands that you have on the world around you?

So if you go into your work place where there are many things you have to do with people, there are many areas where you will obviously step on each other's toes. There is no other way to work.

If there are joyful human beings, the opportunity to touch and mingle with each other will be there; it will be a great opportunity to take this forward in a big way. If miserable people come together, everything is a problem; their very existence is a problem.

People are miserable because they are absolutely inflexible when they are miserable. But the moment you are happy, you are very, very flexible. Isn't it?

People are miserable because they are absolutely inflexible when they are miserable. But the moment you are happy, you are very, very flexible.

No action inside

Arya had this little plastic toy that would make different kinds of sounds when it was squeezed. It worked with air being squeezed out differently each time. Arya would just open up the toy and look inside but he never found anything inside. It looked very quiet in there.

He wondered how the toy could make such sounds outside when there was a quiet inside?

Sadhguru: In terms of just activity in my life, I have probably done more activity than what people would do in 3 lifetimes. I don't just mean the number of things that I have done in my life, even, you know not after I have taken up all this work. I am saying just in terms of activity.

People always think 'where did I get the time to do all this?' You can do so much because you have no issues within yourself. When you have issues within yourself all the time, you know settling this person takes an enormous amount of time and energy. What will you do about the outside? Very little. Action is about the outside, not about the inside. Inside does not need any action, inside is absolute. Only, if only you are in touch with it.

Right now you are all outside. You don't know anything of the inside. Why you do not know Joy fundamentally is because you do not know what is inside. I am not saying in terms of you do not know what is the content of the inside. I am simply saying you do not know the inside at all.

Everything that you know is outside. Right now you think your thoughts and emotions are inside, but they are not inside. Your physical body is not inside; you gathered it from outside in the form of food. What you call as your physical body is just a piece of earth that you gathered.

One day when you fall dead, it'll just become part of the earth once again. Just look at this, all the billions and billions of people who existed on this planet before you and me, where are they? They are all just topsoil, and so will you be. So will your body be one day, unless somebody buries you real deep (laughs). In the ashram, we will do that. We will bury you real deep, because we don't want you to come up again – rise from the dead and bother us (laughs). When you are dead we want you really dead (laughs).

So all these countless number of people of the past have become topsoil. What you call as 'my body' is just an accumulation that you have gathered. What you call as 'my mind' is an accumulation of impressions. So, all this is from the outside. Do you know what is the inside? You don't know any inside; inside is yet to happen to you. That is why Joy is yet to happen to you, because Joy is of the inner nature. Joy is not of the outside.

Once in a way, when certain situations work out for you the way you want them, the inside finds a little expression, just a whiff of fragrance of Joy. If you know the interior, it is a boundless sense of Joy; it is not just a whiff. It is not a fragrance, it is the real thing, and you drown in it.

Once you are in it, then the outside is just a play for you, you play it whichever way. You can play with life any which way you want, but it will not leave a single scratch upon you. Right now life is leaving you absolutely wounded. By the time they're 20, most people are wounded to such a point that they can never recover again in their lives.

You don't know any inside; inside is yet to happen to you. That is why Joy is yet to happen to you, because Joy is of the inner nature. Joy is not of the outside.

To the hilt

Dev's behaviour at breakfast on Sunday mornings was very strange to Lila. Surprisingly he would enjoy the food served much more than on other days of the week Lila would wonder how come he would enjoy the same dishes a hundred times more when he was relaxed on Sundays? She definitely felt he was having a miserable time at work and at home the other days of the week and therefore breakfast was such an ordeal for him on weekdays.

Sadhguru: If you're joyful, whatever you do, you will do it to the hilt because you have nothing to hold back, nothing to fear, isn't it? You will definitely do it to your fullest capability. When you're not, you have your own issue; you will never do anything 100% in your life.

This doesn't mean that you have become a super human being and can do everything. No. You will function to your fullest capacity; at least what you can do will happen in the world. What you cannot do anyway doesn't happen. Whether you're joyful or miserable, it doesn't happen.

If you're joyful, whatever you do you will do it to the hilt because you have nothing to hold back, nothing to fear, isn't it?

Quick fix

Dev and Arya could just not sleep because there was a din of loud music outside the house. Dev and Arya shut all the windows of their home and the doors of their bedroom and then hoped that the sound would vanish but it just did not.

To their surprise, they found Lila sleeping peacefully in her bed. Arya was surprised too and he took a closer look at his mother. Lila had put on earplugs and gone to sleep while Dev and Arya struggled!

Sadhguru: If you shift from being a compulsive existence to a conscious existence, being joyful won't be an effort. Being joyful will be very natural for you.

Right now, you're a compulsive human being, you're compelled by outside situations constantly, and you're hoping to be joyful; that's hope against hope.

When you are a compulsive person, if you have to be joyful, we will have to fix the whole world the way you want it, and if we fix the world the way you want it, nobody else will be joyful. So it is better you're not joyful.

If you shift from being a compulsive existence to a conscious existence, being joyful won't be an effort.

Advantage Joy

Lila and Arya loved a walk through the market. There were several familiar vendors with various kinds of goods.

An old man was selling some cheap wooden toys. He was known to most children and their mothers too. Children loved buying his toys that he sold at amazingly low prices.

Lila was curious about this. She approached the old man and asked him why he sold the toys at such low prices. Wasn't he feeling exploited?

The old man looked at her and smiled and said "Ma'am, I feel exploited if somebody does not buy these toys!"

Sadhguru: Whichever way you are, joyful or miserable, you could be exploited by somebody.

When somebody gets into a position of advantage, either because of his capability or social situation or something else, it is possible that he could exploit you. It is a possibility in the world, wherever you go. But if you're anyway joyful, exploitation has no impact on you.

So, right now, we're making hundreds of people work in

the ashram without paying them anything. This is actually exploitation in its absolute purity, isn't it? Since people are happily being exploited, there is no issue. If people are exploited against their will, only then there is an issue, isn't it? When people willfully want to be exploited, what is anybody's problem? There is no problem.

A person is willfully exploited only when he makes himself in such a way that his very existence has no self-interest. He's okay whichever way you exploit him, because somewhere he sees that he's so joyful, he cannot be a vested interest. When he has nothing to get from you, where is the need for him to exploit you? But if he's doing something that socially seems like exploitation, there must be a good reason. Otherwise he won't do it.

So, people are willing to be willfully exploited although not all of them understand all these things. However, when somewhere they sense someone, who has no particular need for himself but is doing so much, they feel it is better to be a part of that, rather than be in a place where people have terrible needs of their own. So, exploitation can happen any which way but misery is exploitation by itself.

Now if you're a joyful person, nobody can truly exploit you because exploitation means doing something against your well being. When you're a joyful person, who can do anything against your well being? If they put you to death, you will die joyfully. Nobody can exploit a person who is truly joyous, because no matter what you do to him, it is your loss, not his loss. If you kill him, you lose a joyful being. What does he lose? He loses nothing, he just loses a body that doesn't mean anything to him, at least the pains and the struggles of the body are over for him.

So if you are a truly joyful person, no exploitation can ever touch you. Only a miserable person is constantly thinking as to who will exploit him. For every little action, they think there must be some undercurrent of something else. Do you see this happening?

As people become more miserable, they're constantly afraid that somebody will exploit them. All the time, they're paranoid that somebody will take advantage of them. What is there to take advantage in most people? They've made themselves into such a disadvantage, whichever way they exist, they're at a disadvantage. If you're miserable, are you at an advantage or disadvantage? You've made yourself into a disadvantage, is that not exploitation?

If you're miserable nobody needs to exploit you, everything is exploitation. But if you're joyful, no exploitation can ever touch you, it doesn't matter what they do. Whatever they do, even if they do something stupid to you, they're only demeaning their life, not yours. They cannot demean the life of a person who is truly joyful. You can make a miserable person's life meaningless.

A joyful person's life cannot be made meaningless because he's not looking for any meaning. His existence is beautiful by itself, he's not looking for any meaning in his life, how can you demean his life? How can you exploit his life? You cannot.

You cannot exploit Joy, you can only exploit misery. Exploitation is possible on the planet, only because large numbers of people are miserable, otherwise, there is no exploitation.

If you're anyway joyful, exploitation has no impact on you.

All terrain vehicle

Arya was amazingly good at all kinds of playing things that had wheels including bicycles, roller blades, skateboards and so many more. He loved riding these things and playing the motion with their wheels.

"Dad, I am so good at moving around....with these wheels!" Arya exclaimed to his Dad.

*"Sure son, but you are **not** good at this!" said Dev and he walked around and demonstrated his "walking" to Arya.*

Sadhguru: If human beings are very joyful by their own nature, no religion will exist. That was the reality in this part of the world* where there was no religion, just a culture.

There was no religious code for the Hindus. It was only later, when there was external competition, that they started doing all this. There was just culture, different ways to live and a general understanding that if you live this way, it'll take you here or there, that's all.

---

*India

But there was no proper religion as Christianity and Islam know it today. If human beings are truly joyful, if they have no sense of misery, if they have no sense of shame, if they have no sense of guilt in them, and no sense of fear in them, how many people do you think you will find in the churches, mosques, and temples of the world?

Only the enlightened ones would live in the temples then. Right now enlightened ones don't go anywhere near the temple because the most miserable come there. So religion cannot exist if humanity is truly, truly joyful. The very need for religion would be gone.

After all, the very thing that a religion promises whether it is in a crude way or in a subtle way, is that if you follow a particular tenet, a particular moral code, or if you follow certain guidelines, you will go to heaven where you will be joyful. If you become absolutely joyful right here, as far as you're concerned you're already in heaven, so the need to go anywhere would completely disappear from you. Now the deeper, deeper dimensions of life would manifest themselves, because your longing to be in a particular way is gone, now the natural forces of creation would take effect in you and function in you in a completely different way.

So right now, whatever you generally know as religion in the world is just an attempt, quite a miserable attempt to be joyful.

Joy is not a religion; Joy is the goal of all religion. If you reach the goal, why would you need the vehicle? If you reach the destination, why would you still sit in the vehicle? You naturally get out of it, isn't it?

The kind of Joy that you know is elusive. See, right now you think getting married is Joy, having a baby is Joy, getting a job is Joy, getting a promotion is Joy. These are all definitely elusive. On that level if they're saying it, yes. Now, I'm not talking about that level of Joy because that'll never last, it keeps crashing. If they've grasped that, it is good.

So, if you find some Joy in prayer, that is also elusive, I want you to know that. If you find some Joy in drinking alcohol, it is very elusive. The only thing is if you drink alcohol, you will have to suffer a hangover.

If you pray too much maybe you will have a halo, and it'll be too tight over your head giving you a headache. If you don't get it, it is okay, it is really okay. Retarded people are more joyful.

If human beings are very joyful by their own nature, no religion will exist.

No other way to be

It was almost an entire Sunday gone waste felt Arya, Dev and Lila. They had gone out to most parks for a picnic and every place was either very crowded or it was very sunny.

They finally came back home late afternoon, tired and bored and the three of them just relaxed in their backyard below one of the trees. There was a nice cool breeze blowing in their open yard and they felt most relaxed here.

"It is so nice here mom," shouted Arya "we can just picnic right here!"

Sadhguru: If you look back on the history of our traditions, yoga has always been talking about various types of Joy. Brahmanand means the very creation is Joy.

What you see as the physical or the mental, or what you see, as the physical energies are the surface coat. The deeper core, the source of creation is the very joyfulness. When we say Brahmanand we are talking about the creator himself being a Joy or joyfulness. So when I say the creator is joyfulness, what is the point if the creator is joyful and he's sitting somewhere in heaven?

The creator or what you refer to as the source of creation is not sitting somewhere else. If you look at your own body, from the moment of birth to now, how much has it grown. This growth did not happen because of any external stretching, this happened because the creator is constantly functioning from within.

So the source of creation is within you right now and that is joyfulness. If this fundamental force of creation finds expression in your life, if you allow it to move out, joyfulness is just the only way you can be. There is no other way to be and you have no business to be any other way, really. Other states have become a part of you because you are not in tune with your own core. All the other states that you experience are your mind just going out of control.

One knows misery in his life not because something has gone wrong with his life or because an external circumstance is creating misery. Outside situations can cause physical pain but suffering and misery are always caused because your mind does not do what you want it to do.

If your mind were to take instructions from you, definitely nobody would have to teach you philosophies to choose Joy versus misery. You have the necessary intelligence to choose to be joyful, because 'I want to be joyful' is a fundamental longing in a human being.

The thought 'I want to be joyful' is there in you, not because of some teaching, philosophy, scripture or religion. 'I want to be joyful' is the very basic longing of life itself.

The very life within you is longing to be joyful because the nature of the very fundamental source of creation within you is joyfulness.

> 'I want to be joyful' is the very basic longing of life itself. The very life within you is longing to be joyful because the nature of the very fundamental source of creation within you is joyfulness.

Don't create misery

Dev was trying his hand at carving a shape out of wood. He was finding it quite difficult to carve out a simple looking vase from the wood. He threw his hands up in despair and looked at Lila almost asking her what he should be doing to create a vase from the wood.

"Simple!" exclaimed Lila "remove all the block of wood which is not the vase!" and she laughed.

Sadhguru: Many, many people have just forgotten that there is something called joyfulness. They think Joy is an illusion. They think Joy is a deception of life and that misery is the truth. This is not true.

If you're not entangled with the modifications of your mind, joyfulness is a natural way. Your misery has come because you have lost control over your own mind. You started operating your mind, which is a complex machine and then after some time you don't know where the hell it is going, that's the source of your misery.

Misery is not raining upon you, nor is Joy raining upon you. Both are happening from within you. If you do not create misery, Joy will be a natural state, please see. You don't have to create Joy, if you just know how not to create misery, Joy will naturally be the only thing that will be there. So it is the most basic and natural state.

If you do not create misery, Joy will be a natural state.

Joyless idiots

Why do I have to go to school Mom?" asked Arya one evening when Lila was sitting in her easy chair in their front lawn.

"To learn my dear." was her rather uninterested reply. *"But there is so much to learn here at home Mom, from you and Dad"*

"But at school they will force you to learn son" Lila was a little more involved now with what she was saying.

"But I don't want to be forced Mom when I want to learn..." said Arya looking at his mom.

Sadhguru: Are you aware what the priority of your life is? Why are you doing everything that you are doing?

If you want to go to the ocean and you are going towards it, that's fine; but if your intention is to climb the mountain, but you walk towards the ocean, is it not stupid? Absolutely stupid.

Now, fundamentally, you started every activity in your life in pursuit of your Joy, and on the way you became so unaware that you don't know why the hell you are doing what you are doing. That proves that whatever you consider a priority becomes more important than your being joyful, or making the atmosphere around you joyful. So you create unpleasantness both for yourself and the world around you.

Maybe, see the only reason why you are getting away with it is because a large population is with you. I want you to understand. You have found some credibility in the world only because there are too many idiots like you. Joyless idiots. If the whole world was joyful, and only you were miserable, instantly you would know this is not the way to be. There is a huge atmosphere of joyless people. They all have some reason for being miserable. Even within the ashram, do you see people have many reasons to create misery for themselves? Where is it that you don't have a reason tell me?

For one who wants to find an excuse to make himself miserable, tell me in which part of the world there is no excuse, North Pole or South Pole? Even there, there is an excuse. Everywhere there is an excuse. If there are no human beings, there will still be some excuse for you to make yourself miserable. So, it doesn't matter why you are miserable. There is no such thing as why you are miserable; there is no other reason except that you don't have any life sense.

Your life is longing to become joyful but your mind and emotions are going somewhere else. Your intention is to go this way while your life energies want to go the other way. Now you are obviously a mess. You will obviously be a torture. No other way to be. You do everything wrong and you hope that the right things will happen. Such things don't happen.

For ages and ages, they have been telling you to look up to God and 'right things will happen' but they have not happened. I want you to look at this very carefully. Only those people who did the right things with their life, those things worked out, and those aspects of life worked out for them. Maybe they built their confidence with God or they sought somebody's help.

You seek anybody's help, I don't care, but unless you do the right thing, the results won't happen in this world. That is the law of nature. This is the fundamental law of nature whether it is interior or exterior. Unless you take appropriate action there will be no results.

Your life is longing to become joyful. Your mind is going somewhere and your emotion is going somewhere else. Your intention is to go this way while your life energies want to go the other way. Now you are obviously a mess.

Nobody is a layman

"How do you manage to tire yourself like this everyday Dev?"
Lila asked him one evening when she saw him dragging himself
lifelessly into the house.

"Well you don't have to do much my dear..." he huffed and
puffed " you just have to enter the office and then you are on
auto pilot, by end of the day the damn machine-of- an- office
just tires you almost surely!"

Sadhguru: Nobody is a layman. Everybody is an absolute
expert in creating misery and suffering for himself and
everybody around him isn't it? Each one of them could be
the CEO of hell because they're such experts at torturing
themselves, but if you're bidding they'll all lose.

So, they're not laymen, they've invested their life in
misery. They just have to understand, it is stupid to do
that. If intelligence functions, naturally you would invest
your life towards Joy, not towards misery. Misery is your
creation.

Joy is not your creation; it is a part of the existing
creation. If you stop creating your nonsense, Joy is the

only way. That's why there are no CEOs in heaven because it doesn't need any management. Misery needs management, Joy doesn't. If you don't mess with anything, you're joyful.

> *Misery needs management, Joy doesn't. If you don't mess with anything, you're joyful.*

Standard format

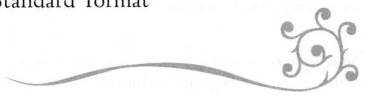

Lila had been reading her favourite author's novels since she was 6 years old. She just loved them. She had carefully preserved a few dozens of these novels and she would read them again and again. Dev found this rather stupid — how can she enjoy them each time, he wondered.

One day he was laughing at Lila who seemed to be enjoying her favourite author. Lila looked at him and asked him why he was laughing himself silly.

Dev laughed and paused and said, "Are you enjoying your author Lila?"

"Why of course yes!" she said looking at him with curiosity.

Dev laughed uncontrollably, holding his stomach and said "Well! The book that you are holding has your favourite author on the cover but the text inside is not by that author, I did this just to fool you!"

Sadhguru: How or, why should the society even know whether you're joyous or not? It is an inner experience. If you've made your joyousness a particular type of expression, like always grinning, then yes, somebody will knock you on your head, and say 'Stop the grin man', okay? When he's going through something and if you keep on grinning, he will break your face so that you can't grin again.

So if you have no such issues, you know how to be in any situation and still be joyful within you, why would the society have anything to do with it? So now, because your Joy finds a particular expression, it is a problem. If your expression is conscious, not compulsive, you can be dead serious and be absolutely joyful within.

It is not an act; you need to understand Joy is not seeking any particular expression. You have chosen certain expressions because you identify those expressions with what you think is joyfulness. As you have thought certain activity will bring Joy, you also think Joy will find expression in a certain way. Not necessarily. It can find expression as it is there, as it is necessary for the situation.

Being joyful means you have absolutely no compulsions of your own anymore. Once you have no compulsions, being the way the situation demands is not at all an effort for you, isn't it? Right now if everybody is mourning here, you can be a more serious mourner than anybody but be absolutely untouched by it.

You don't feel any loss, but you can still go through the mourning period more gracefully than others. That's the freedom that Joy gives you, it takes away all compulsions. Misery is the basis of compulsions; please see, because you're afraid of being miserable, you're compelled to act in a particular way. You're compelled to eat in a particular way, do things in a particular way and be in a particular way because you're afraid if you don't do that, you will become miserable.

Once that possibility is taken off, you can be any way, as the situation demands, because there's no compulsiveness in you because your Joy is never under threat. So, why would the society be against your Joy?

When you're joyful, you have absolutely no compulsions of your own anymore. Once you have no compulsions, it is not an effort for you to be the way the situation demands, isn't it?

Don't worry, be happy

There was a young and bright colleague of Dev who was also very energetic and creative.

He found that on Saturdays when the office worked for just a few hours, everyone was at their relaxed best and were comfortable with each other.

He boldly went to the manager and convinced him to drive a massive communication campaign which said "EVERYDAY IS A SATURDAY HERE!"

The manager liked the idea and promptly agreed to splash this message all over.

Slowly however everyone started behaving as if it were a Saturday every day — they were relaxed and focussed on the objective and there were fewer conflicts around.

However the manager soon noticed a major problem. Employees started leaving early for home. They were assuming it to be a Saturday with fewer working hours. So he immediately stopped the campaign.

Sadhguru: 'Don't worry, be happy, don't worry, be happy',

this did not work because you tried to make it a slogan in your life.

How can you not worry about things that you're concerned about? The moment you tell yourself 'do not worry and be happy', obviously, you have a situation within you where your mind gets into a state of repetitive thought process beyond your control, that's worry, isn't it?

Worrying means going on thinking about the same nonsense. Thinking about something is not worrying, you better think about things clearly, but going on thinking about the same thing is worry. That means your mind works like a scratched record disc, which plays the same thing, over and over again.

Obviously, if your mind has become like this, that means it is not in good shape, isn't it? Some situation in life may have caused an abrasion in your mind as a result of which, your mind plays like a scratched record disc, playing the same thing, again, and again, and again. Wherever you go it says the same thing.

So, instead of fixing the record disc, or switching off the record player, you have now changed it into a different tune. Instead of saying one kind of line, you have started saying a new line. Initially, it looks like it works, but after some time, you will feel deep frustrations.

People have been trying to teach you what at one time was popularly known as positive thinking – 'don't worry, be happy', 'no matter what's happening, it is all for the good', 'I'm okay you're okay, everything will be okay'. Life hasn't yet got you.

The very apostles of positive thinking lost their minds; they even committed suicide because it only works initially, to some extent. It will not work with all aspects of life, this must be clear. Except the fundamental truth that is the very basis of this existence, that nothing works on all levels of life. You can bullshit yourself into well being in so many different ways, but it'll not last.

So, this is the reason why people said God is the only way. When they said God, they were not talking about your god, my god, this god, that god, or some fool who is sitting up there. God means the basis of your creation. Right now, in your experience, where is the basis of your creation, within or outside? Definitely within, isn't it? The very growth of this body is happening from within. So the basis of creation is within you, that's exactly what I'm saying. The core of your existence right now, which is the basis of your creation, is Joy: that's the only way.

The moment you tell yourself 'do not worry and be happy', obviously, you have a situation within you where your mind gets into a state of repetitive thought process beyond your control, that's worry, isn't it?

The way out

An old man was standing at the crossroad near a small quaint downtown area that had a lot of little lanes that Dev had not visited much.

"I am lost sir, what is the way out of here?" Dev asked him peering out of his car window.

"Way out?" laughed the old man "that depends on where you want to go out to. But I bet you know the way in, young man!"

Sadhguru: How you experience Joy is not the point. At that moment whichever way you experience it, it is true. When people call it elusive, what they mean is that it is momentary, you can't hold it, it keeps crashing and that there is no permanence to it. So, people talk about eternal Joy in heaven.

Have you ever experienced anything called as past or future? You remember the past, you imagine the future but your experience of life has always been in this moment. Right now you are in this moment, tomorrow you will be in this moment, hundred years later if you exist you'll be in this moment, a million years later if you exist you will still be in this moment.

So, this moment is eternity. So, don't look for a way out, there is only one way; 'Way in'. There is no 'way out'. Once you become life, there is no way out, but there's a way in and that's why the struggle. People always think of a way out, there's no 'way out', there's only 'way in'.

You always thought if you open the door and go out that's freedom, but you don't realize that the door that leads you inside is freedom. That's the struggle, that's the whole struggle of all the people. They're always thinking of a way out. No way out, you can't opt out of life, even if you commit suicide, one more body will form around you, one more and one more, and one more.

There's only a way in, you find that way in and you're out. This is going out through the in-door, you understand? If you try to go out through the out-door, it is never going to happen, this is out through the in-door.

> *Don't look for a way out,*
> *there is only one way;*
> *'Way in'. There is no 'way out'*

Joy is here!

Joy is here!

Dev did not seem too satisfied about his work over the years. He had tried different jobs in different companies and industries and found no great change in his job satisfaction. He had also worked in a couple of different locations and he found that the change he experienced was not much in the way he was feeling about them.

Lila did not have much to say about Dev's jobs and how he felt about them. She felt that "his nature" was so much the problem and not where he worked or what he did and this was the cause of his dissatisfaction with his work.

One evening as they were chatting in the living room, they saw Arya playing with a couple of broken toys by the passage and he was enjoying them. He had also enjoyed the set of new toys he played with the previous evening. What toy he played with seemed immaterial. It suddenly struck Dev that it was "not about the toy" but so much about "how Arya played with them"

He smiled and looked at Lila like never before. Lila looked at Dev and smiled back and with this strong feeling this was the beginning of something new, something tremendous that was to happen to Dev.........

Sadhguru: On a certain day, three men were working in one place. A man passing that way stopped and asked the first man, 'what are you doing here?' The first man said, 'why, are you blind, can't you see? I am cutting stone.' He was actually cutting stone. He went to the second man and asked, 'what are you doing here?'

That man said, 'I'm doing something to fill my belly.' He then went to the third man and asked, 'what are you doing here?' That man stood up in great Joy and said, 'I am building a wonderful temple here.' All three men were doing the same work. In one person's experience he was just cutting stone, in another's he was just filling his belly and in the third person's experience he was creating a wonderful temple.

So the quality of your life will change not by changing the content of your life, it will change only by changing the context of your life. When we say 'no expectation or taking away the calculation', we are not talking about you living on the streets like a beggar. We are just talking about changing the context not the content. By changing the content nothing changes. By changing the clothes that you wear, food that you eat, the place that you live, the quality of your life will not change, isn't it? If you move from your home to the ashram, you will have more problems there than at home, because if you were having problems with four people at home, do you know how many problems you will have with 1000 people in the ashram? Yes? So, it is not the content that you need to change, it is the context of your life that you need to change.

You can go to your office because you really want to contribute to what's happening there. So if you function in this manner, won't they give you a salary at the end of the month? They will pay you, isn't it? But for 30 days if you keep chanting 'salary, salary, salary', you will be miserable for 30 days hoping for that one day to come and on that one day you will be even more miserable because it doesn't matter how much salary you get, it's never enough, isn't it? Does anybody get enough salary on this planet? Nobody gets enough, isn't it? There is no such thing as enough salary — it is always insufficient. Yes. That's because as your salary increases, your lifestyle is already two steps ahead of that. So the question is not about what you do or what you do not do — how you do it changes life.

"Joy will not happen if you change the Content of your life, it will only happen if you change the Context of your life"

Epilogue

A Joyful Experience

This happened to me a couple of weeks before the Samyama (8 day silence program offered by Sadhguru) for which I was preparing during the month of January. I had finished my morning kriyas which I was initiated by Sadhguru including Shaktichalan Kriya and the Shambhavi Maha Mudra.

As I was driving to work, I felt I was flying. Flying with rapture and Joy. There was Joy all through me – through my body, my mind, my emotion – just all over me. It was completely inexplicable and I could not really describe how I felt.

As the day moved on at work, the Joy seemed to continue. I felt as if my body was being constantly charged by a 1,000 volt power battery with receptors all over at various points. The source of this battery seemed to be "inside me" but I just could not locate or identify where this was.

This Joy felt so much like "giving" to people and the world around rather than "wanting". At different points of the day it seemed to just not have any desires really but it just seemed to be there "by itself". I felt I was just going absolutely crazy since I could not really describe to anyone what this was about and neither did I know why it was happening. Every moment seemed to be gliding and I was so much there to experience it. There was Joy bursting all over inside me and I just wanted to run around and share it with everyone and just give it away as if there an endless supply source inside me that I could give it away to whoever I knew or was around me.

I was flying around wherever I was almost like a zombie. I was too scared (with Joy!) about what people would think if I told them what was happening inside me.

Everything that I saw or did seemed to be "joyful". I had never perceived things, people and situations like I perceived that day. The Joy was so well "glued" inside that it looked like nothing would shake it out. It did not depend on an "externality" to happen for it to continue. It was just "on" by itself.

At some point this Joy felt so complete and by itself that I almost felt that I could just lie down right there and be ready to die joyfully. The ecstasy was so much full of life that it looked like death was trivial.

That day it surely looked to me that being Joyful every moment, everyday was a definite possibility this very lifetime. This was just one grand day of being fully Joyful that I had experienced – imagine a whole lifetime of being joyful.

I do not know how this can happen or when this would happen but now I know it "can happen".

May this happen to you – everyday of your life!

— (Jeetendra Jain)

For more see www.joy24x7.com

Isha Foundation

Isha Foundation is a non-religious, not-for-profit, public service organization that addresses all aspects of human well-being. From its powerful yoga programs for inner transformation to its inspiring social and environmental projects, Isha activities are designed to create an inclusive culture as a basis for global peace and development.

This integral approach has gained worldwide recognition, as reflected in Isha Foundation's Special Consultative Status with the Economic and Social Council (ECOSOC) of the United Nations. Hundreds of thousands of volunteers support the Foundation's work in over 200 centers across the globe.

Sadhguru

A profound mystic and visionary humanitarian, Sadhguru is a spiritual Master with a difference. An arresting blend of profundity and pragmatism, his life and work serve as a reminder that inner sciences are not esoteric disciplines from an outdated past, but vitally relevant to our times.

With speaking engagements that take him around the world, Sadhguru is widely sought after by prestigious global forums such as the United Nations Millennium Peace Summit, the Australian Leadership Retreat and the World Economic Forum.

Isha Yoga Programs

Isha Yoga offers a unique possibility for individuals to empower themselves and reach their full potential. Designed by Sadhguru to suit individuals from every social and cultural background, Isha Yoga programs extend a rare opportunity for self-discovery and inner transformation under the guidance of an enlightened Master.

Isha Yoga Center

Isha Yoga Center, founded under the aegis of Isha Foundation, is located at the Velliangiri Foothills amidst a forest reserve with abundant wildlife. Created as a powerful center for inner growth, this popular destination attracts people from all parts of the world.

Dhyanalinga Yogic Temple

The Dhyanalinga is a powerful and unique energy form, the essence of yogic sciences. The Dhyanalinga Yogic Temple is a meditative space that does not ascribe to any particular faith or belief system nor requires any ritual, prayer or worship. The vibrational energies of the Dhyanalinga allow even those unaware of meditation to experience a deep state of meditativeness, revealing the essential nature of life.

Isha Rejuvenation

Isha Rejuvenation offers unique, carefully scientifically structured programs designed by Sadhguru to bring vibrancy and optimal balance to one's life energies, thus facilitating healthy living as well as the prevention and uprooting of chronic ailments.

Action for Rural Rejuvenation

Action for Rural Rejuvenation (ARR) is a holistic social outreach program whose primary objective is to improve the overall health and quality of life of the rural poor.

Dedicated teams of qualified and trained personnel operate ARR's Mobile Health Clinics, which currently provide free basic health care to more than 4,000 villages in South India.

Project GreenHands

Project GreenHands (PGH) is an ecological initiative of Isha Foundation to prevent and reverse environmental degradation and enable sustainable living. The project aims to create 10% additional green cover in Tamil Nadu. Drawing on the participation of a wide cross-section of people, 114 million trees will be planted by the year 2010.

Isha Vidhya – An Isha Education Initiative

Isha Vidhya provides affordable, high quality primary school education to villages across South India's Tamil Nadu state. Over the coming years, Isha Vidhya will set up 206 schools designed specifically to create confident, English-speaking, computer literate children. Students will graduate prepared to pursue higher education.

Isha Home School

Isha Home School, set in the tranquil surroundings of the Velliangiri Foothills, offers a stimulating environment for the inner blossoming of each child. Isha Home School helps each student reach his or her true potential and enhances his or her natural and latent talents while maintaining high standards of academic excellence.

Isha Business

Isha Business is a venture spearheaded and promoted by Isha Foundation to bring a touch of Isha into people's lives through numerous products and services, such as architectural and interior design, construction, furniture, crafts, clothing and much more. The proceeds benefit the poorest of the poor through Action for Rural Rejuvenation.

Contact Us:

INDIA

Isha Yoga Center
Velliangiri Foothills
Semmedu (P.O.)
Coimbatore-641 114, India
Tel. +91-422-2515345
info@ishafoundation.org

USA

Isha Foundation Inc./Isha Institute of Inner Sciences
951, Isha Lane
McMinnville, TN-37110, USA
Tel: +1-866-424-ISHA (4742)
usa@ishafoundation.org

UNITED KINGDOM

Isha Institute of Inner Sciences
PO Box 559,
Isleworth, TW7 5WR, UK
Tel: +44-7956998729
uk@ishafoundation.org

For more information on your local center, please visit our website:

www.ishafoundation.org

Dhyanalinga — The Silent Revolution

This richly illustrated book presents a deeper definition of yoga and its metaphysical essence. It culminates in the presentation of the Dhyanalinga.

Encounter the Enlightened — Conversations with the Master

This book captures interactive moments with the Master. It is an invitation to the reader to go beyond words and experience the wisdom of the boundless.

Eternal Echoes — The Sacred sounds through the Mystic

A compelling and provocative collection of poetry by Sadhguru. This book of high artistic merit moves us into the timeless, eternal reality of an enlightened being.

Flowers on the Path

A compilation of articles created by Sadhguru for the Speaking Tree column of the Times of India. These articles bring infusions of beauty, humor, clarity and insight into our lives.

Midnights with the Mystic – A Little Guide to Freedom and Bliss

Presented in a series of conversations between seeker, the co-author Cheryl Simone, and enlightened Master, Sadhguru, this captivating book challenges us to embrace the possibility of a higher reality, a peak of consciousness. Available at bookstores and online booksellers such as amazon.com and Barnes & Noble.

Find further inspiration in Sadhguru's profound insights on a variety of life-relevant topics, combined in pairs of two in the following revealing books:

- Enlightenment: What It Is & Leave Death Alone
- Dissolving Your Personality & Good and Bad Divides the World
- Ancient Technology for the Modern Mind & Culture of Peace
- Dimension Beyond the Physical & Circus of the Intellect
- Living Life to the Fullest & Unleashing the Mind
- Is Spirituality a Science & Isha: Sacred Space for Self Transformation

Joy 24 x 7

Visit www.joy24x7.com